MW00623459

Black Letter Series

of

WEST PUBLISHING COMPANY

P.O. Box 64526

St. Paul, Minnesota 55164–0526

Accounting

FARIS' ACCOUNTING AND LAW IN A NUTSHELL, 377 pages, 1984. Softcover. (Text)

Administrative Law

GELLHORN AND LEVIN'S ADMINISTRATIVE LAW AND PROCESS IN A NUTSHELL, Third Edition, 479 pages, 1990. Softcover. (Text)

Admiralty

MARAIST'S ADMIRALTY IN A NUTSHELL, Second Edition, 379 pages, 1988. Softcover. (Text)

SCHOENBAUM'S HORNBOOK ON ADMIRALTY AND MARITIME LAW, Student Edition, 692 pages, 1987 with 1989 pocket part. (Text)

Agency—Partnership

REUSCHLEIN AND GREGORY'S HORNBOOK ON THE LAW OF AGENCY AND PARTNERSHIP, Second Edition, 683 pages, 1990. (Text)

STEFFEN'S AGENCY-PARTNERSHIP IN A NUTSHELL, 364 pages, 1977. Softcover. (Text)

American Indian Law

CANBY'S AMERICAN INDIAN LAW IN A NUTSHELL, Second Edition, 336 pages, 1988. Softcover. (Text)

Antitrust—see also Regulated Industries, Trade Regulation

GELLHORN'S ANTITRUST LAW AND ECONOMICS IN A NUTSHELL, Third Edition, 472 pages,

Antitrust—Continued

1986. Softcover. (Text)

HOVENKAMP'S BLACK LETTER ON ANTITRUST, 323 pages, 1986. Softcover. (Review)

HOVENKAMP'S HORNBOOK ON ECONOMICS AND FEDERAL ANTITRUST LAW, Student Edition, 414 pages, 1985. (Text)

SULLIVAN'S HORNBOOK OF THE LAW OF ANTITRUST, 886 pages, 1977. (Text)

Appellate Advocacy—see Trial and Appellate Advocacy

Art Law

DUBOFF'S ART LAW IN A NUTSHELL, 335 pages, 1984. Softcover. (Text)

Banking Law

LOVETT'S BANKING AND FINANCIAL INSTITUTIONS LAW IN A NUTSHELL, Second Edition, 464 pages, 1988. Softcover. (Text)

Civil Procedure—see also Federal Jurisdiction and Procedure

CLERMONT'S BLACK LETTER ON CIVIL PROCEDURE, Second Edition, 332 pages, 1988. Softcover. (Review)

FRIEDENTHAL, KANE AND MILLER'S HORNBOOK ON CIVIL PROCEDURE, 876 pages, 1985.

(Text)

KANE'S CIVIL PROCEDURE IN A NUTSHELL, Third Edition, 303 pages, 1991. Softcover. (Text)

KOFFLER AND REPPY'S HORNBOOK ON COMMON LAW PLEADING, 663 pages, 1969. (Text)

SIEGEL'S HORNBOOK ON NEW YORK PRACTICE, Second Edition, Student Edition, 1068 pages, 1991. Softcover. (Text)

Commercial Law

BAILEY AND HAGEDORN'S SECURED TRANSACTIONS IN A NUTSHELL, Third Edition, 390 pages, 1988. Softcover. (Text)

HENSON'S HORNBOOK ON SECURED TRANSACTIONS UNDER THE U.C.C., Second Edition, 504 pages, 1979, with 1979 pocket part. (Text)

NICKLES' BLACK LETTER ON COMMERCIAL PAPER, 450 pages, 1988. Softcover. (Review)

SPEIDEL'S BLACK LETTER ON SALES AND SALES FINANCING, 363 pages, 1984. Softcover. (Review)

STOCKTON'S SALES IN A NUTSHELL, Second Edition, 370 pages, 1981. Softcover. (Text)

Commercial Law—Continued

STONE'S UNIFORM COMMERCIAL CODE IN A NUTSHELL, Third Edition, 580 pages, 1989. Softcover. (Text)

WEBER AND SPEIDEL'S COMMERCIAL PAPER IN A NUTSHELL, Third Edition, 404 pages, 1982. Softcover. (Text)

WHITE AND SUMMERS' HORNBOOK ON THE UNIFORM COMMERCIAL CODE, Third Edition, Student Edition, 1386 pages, 1988. (Text)

Community Property

MENNELL AND BOYKOFF'S COMMUNITY PROPERTY IN A NUTSHELL, Second Edition, 432 pages, 1988. Softcover. (Text)

Comparative Law

GLENDON, GORDON AND OSAKWE'S COMPARATIVE LEGAL TRADITIONS IN A NUTSHELL. 402 pages, 1982. Softcover. (Text)

Conflict of Laws

HAY'S BLACK LETTER ON CONFLICT OF LAWS, 330 pages, 1989. Softcover. (Review)

SCOLES AND HAY'S HORNBOOK ON CONFLICT OF LAWS, Student Edition, approximately 1025 pages, 1992. (Text)

SIEGEL'S CONFLICTS IN A NUTSHELL, 470 pages, 1982. Softcover. (Text)

Constitutional Law—Civil Rights

BARRON AND DIENES' BLACK LETTER ON CONSTITUTIONAL LAW, Third Edition, 440 pages, 1991. Softcover. (Review)

BARRON AND DIENES' CONSTITUTIONAL LAW IN A NUTSHELL, Second Edition, 483 pages, 1991. Softcover. (Text)

ENGDAHL'S CONSTITUTIONAL FEDERALISM IN A NUTSHELL, Second Edition, 411 pages, 1987. Softcover. (Text)

MARKS AND COOPER'S STATE CONSTITUTIONAL LAW IN A NUTSHELL, 329 pages, 1988. Softcover. (Text)

NOWAK AND ROTUNDA'S HORNBOOK ON CONSTITUTIONAL LAW, Fourth Edition, 1357 pages, 1991. (Text)

VIEIRA'S CONSTITUTIONAL CIVIL RIGHTS IN A NUTSHELL, Second Edition, 322 pages, 1990. Softcover. (Text)

WILLIAMS' CONSTITUTIONAL ANALYSIS IN A NUTSHELL, 388 pages, 1979. Softcover. (Text)

Consumer Law—see also Commercial Law

EPSTEIN AND NICKLES' CONSUMER LAW IN A NUTSHELL, Second Edition, 418 pages, 1981. Softcover. (Text)

Contracts

CALAMARI AND PERILLO'S BLACK LETTER ON CONTRACTS, Second Edition, 462 pages, 1990. Softcover. (Review)

CALAMARI AND PERILLO'S HORNBOOK ON CONTRACTS, Third Edition, 1049 pages, 1987. (Text)

CORBIN'S TEXT ON CONTRACTS, One Volume Student Edition, 1224 pages, 1952. (Text)

FRIEDMAN'S CONTRACT REMEDIES IN A NUTSHELL, 323 pages, 1981. Softcover. (Text)

KEYES' GOVERNMENT CONTRACTS IN A NUTSHELL, Second Edition, 557 pages, 1990. Softcover. (Text)

SCHABER AND ROHWER'S CONTRACTS IN A NUTSHELL, Third Edition, 457 pages, 1990. Softcover. (Text)

Copyright—see Patent and Copyright Law

Corporations

HAMILTON'S BLACK LETTER ON CORPORATIONS, Second Edition, 513 pages, 1986. Softcover. (Review)

HAMILTON'S THE LAW OF CORPORATIONS IN A NUTSHELL, Third Edition, 518 pages, 1991. Softcover. (Text)

HENN AND ALEXANDER'S HORNBOOK ON LAWS OF CORPORATIONS, Third Edition, Student Edition, 1371 pages, 1983, with 1986 pocket part. (Text)

Corrections

KRANTZ' THE LAW OF CORRECTIONS AND PRISONERS' RIGHTS IN A NUTSHELL, Third Edition, 407 pages, 1988. Softcover. (Text)

Creditors' Rights

EPSTEIN'S DEBTOR-CREDITOR LAW IN A NUTSHELL, Fourth Edition, 401 pages, 1991. Softcover. (Text)

NICKLES AND EPSTEIN'S BLACK LETTER ON CREDITORS' RIGHTS AND BANKRUPTCY, 576 pages, 1989. (Review)

Criminal Law and Criminal Procedure—see also Corrections, Juvenile Justice

ISRAEL AND LAFAVE'S CRIMINAL PROCEDURE—CONSTITUTIONAL LIMITATIONS IN A NUTSHELL, Fourth Edition, 461 pages, 1988. Softcover. (Text)

LAFAVE AND ISRAEL'S HORN-

Criminal Law and Criminal Procedure—Continued

BOOK ON CRIMINAL PROCEDURE, Second Edition, approximately 1350 pages, 1992. (Text)

LAFAVE AND SCOTT'S HORNBOOK ON CRIMINAL LAW, Second Edition, 918 pages, 1986. (Text)

LOEWY'S CRIMINAL LAW IN A NUTSHELL, Second Edition, 321 pages, 1987. Softcover. (Text)

LOW'S BLACK LETTER ON CRIMINAL LAW, Revised First Edition, 443 pages, 1990. Softcover. (Review)

Domestic Relations

CLARK'S HORNBOOK ON DOMESTIC RELATIONS, Second Edition, Student Edition, 1050 pages, 1988. (Text)

KRAUSE'S BLACK LETTER ON FAMILY LAW, 314 pages, 1988. Softcover. (Review)

KRAUSE'S FAMILY LAW IN A NUTSHELL, Second Edition, 444 pages, 1986. Softcover. (Text)

MALLOY'S LAW AND ECONOMICS: A COMPARATIVE APPROACH TO THEORY AND PRACTICE, 166 pages, 1990. Softcover. (Text)

Education Law

ALEXANDER AND ALEXANDER'S THE LAW OF SCHOOLS, STUDENTS AND TEACHERS IN A NUTSHELL, 409 pages, 1984. Softcover. (Text)

Employment Discrimination—see also Gender Discrimination

PLAYER'S FEDERAL LAW OF EMPLOYMENT DISCRIMINATION IN A NUTSHELL, Third Edition, approximately 270 pages, 1992. Softcover. (Text)

PLAYER'S HORNBOOK ON EMPLOYMENT DISCRIMINATION LAW, Student Edition, 708 pages, 1988. (Text)

Energy and Natural Resources Law—see also Oil and Gas

LAITOS AND TOMAIN'S ENERGY AND NATURAL RESOURCES LAW IN A NUTSHELL, Approximately 525 pages, 1992. Softcover. (Text)

Environmental Law—see also Energy and Natural Resources Law; Sea, Law of

FINDLEY AND FARBER'S ENVIRONMENTAL LAW IN A NUTSHELL, Third Edition, approximately 375 pages, February, 1992 Pub. Softcover. (Text)

RODGERS' HORNBOOK ON ENVIRONMENTAL LAW, 956 pages,

Professional Responsibility—
Continued

IN A NUTSHELL, Second Edition, 514 pages, 1991. Softcover. (Text)

ROTUNDA'S BLACK LETTER ON PROFESSIONAL RESPONSIBILITY, Third Edition, approximately 400 pages, 1992. Softcover. (Review)

WOLFRAM'S HORNBOOK ON MODERN LEGAL ETHICS, Student Edition, 1120 pages, 1986. (Text)

Property—see also Real Estate Transactions, Land Use, Trusts and Estates

BERNHARDT'S BLACK LETTER ON PROPERTY, Second Edition, 388 pages, 1991. Softcover. (Review)

BERNHARDT'S REAL PROPERTY IN A NUTSHELL, Second Edition, 448 pages, 1981. Softcover. (Text)

BOYER, HOVENKAMP AND KURTZ' THE LAW OF PROPERTY, AN INTRODUCTORY SURVEY, Fourth Edition, 696 pages, 1991. (Text)

BURKE'S PERSONAL PROPERTY IN A NUTSHELL, 322 pages, 1983. Softcover. (Text)

CUNNINGHAM, STOEBUCK AND WHITMAN'S HORNBOOK ON THE

LAW OF PROPERTY, Student Edition, 916 pages, 1984, with 1987 pocket part. (Text)

HILL'S LANDLORD AND TENANT LAW IN A NUTSHELL, Second Edition, 311 pages, 1986. Softcover. (Text)

Real Estate Transactions

BRUCE'S REAL ESTATE FINANCE IN A NUTSHELL, Third Edition, 287 pages, 1991. Softcover. (Text)

NELSON AND WHITMAN'S BLACK LETTER ON LAND TRANSACTIONS AND FINANCE, Second Edition, 466 pages, 1988. Softcover. (Review)

NELSON AND WHITMAN'S HORNBOOK ON REAL ESTATE FINANCE LAW, Second Edition, 941 pages, 1985 with 1989 pocket part. (Text)

Regulated Industries—see also Mass Communication Law, Banking Law

GELLHORN AND PIERCE'S REGULATED INDUSTRIES IN A NUTSHELL, Second Edition, 389 pages, 1987. Softcover. (Text)

Remedies

DOBBS' HORNBOOK ON REMEDIES, 1067 pages, 1973. (Text)

DOBBYN'S INJUNCTIONS IN A NUTSHELL, 264 pages, 1974.

Taxation—Individual—Continued

NUTSHELL, Fourth Edition, 503 pages, 1988. Softcover. (Text)

POSIN'S HORNBOOK ON FEDERAL INCOME TAXATION, Student Edition, 491 pages, 1983, with 1989 pocket part. (Text)

ROSE AND CHOMMIE'S HORNBOOK ON FEDERAL INCOME TAXATION, Third Edition, 923 pages, 1988, with 1991 pocket part. (Text)

Taxation—International

DOERNBERG'S INTERNATIONAL TAXATION IN A NUTSHELL, 325 pages, 1989. Softcover. (Text)

BISHOP AND BROOKS' FEDERAL PARTNERSHIP TAXATION: A GUIDE TO THE LEADING CASES, STATUTES, AND REGULATIONS, 545 pages, 1990. Softcover. (Text)

BURKE'S FEDERAL INCOME TAXATION OF PARTNERSHIPS IN A NUTSHELL, Approximately 400 pages, February, 1992 Pub. Softcover. (Text)

SCHWARZ AND LATHROPE'S BLACK LETTER ON CORPORATE AND PARTNERSHIP TAXATION, 537 pages, 1991. Softcover. (Review)

Taxation—State & Local

GELFAND AND SALSICH'S STATE AND LOCAL TAXATION AND FINANCE IN A NUTSHELL, 309 pages, 1986. Softcover. (Text)

Torts—see also Products Liability

KIONKA'S BLACK LETTER ON TORTS, 339 pages, 1988. Softcover. (Review)

KIONKA'S TORTS IN A NUTSHELL, Second Edition, approximately 500 pages, March, 1992 Pub. Softcover. (Text)

MALONE'S TORTS IN A NUTSHELL: INJURIES TO FAMILY, SOCIAL AND TRADE RELATIONS, 358 pages, 1979. Softcover. (Text)

PROSSER AND KEETON'S HORNBOOK ON TORTS, Fifth Edition, Student Edition, 1286 pages, 1984 with 1988 pocket part. (Text)

Trade Regulation—see also Antitrust, Regulated Industries

McMANIS' UNFAIR TRADE PRACTICES IN A NUTSHELL, Second Edition, 464 pages, 1988. Softcover. (Text)

SCHECHTER'S BLACK LETTER ON UNFAIR TRADE PRACTICES, 272 pages, 1986. Softcover. (Re-

Advisory Board

[XIV]

INJUNCTIONS
IN A NUTSHELL

By

JOHN F. DOBBYN
Professor of Law, Villanova Law School

ST. PAUL, MINN.
WEST PUBLISHING CO.
1974

Dobbyn—Injunct.Nutshell
7th Reprint—1992

∞

TO LOIS

My Bride, Friend, and Partner

*

III

PREFACE

No area of the law can surpass the subject of the equitable remedy of injunctions for bringing the legal process into personal contact with the entire span of human frictions. It is among the most ancient *and* most modern forms of relief available through our legal system; and it continues to grow with every new area of personal or business interest that achieves recognition by court or legislature. When the field of civil rights expanded into prominence, the need for a remedy that would give practical meaning to the concept was met by injunctions. The same was true in the area of newly recognized rights to protection against unfair business competition and invasions of privacy. Today, the beginnings of inroads into the complex problems of pollution are being made by means of injunctions. It has proven to be a remedy that is imaginative and flexible enough to follow the substantive law into any avenue it chooses to take.

The purpose of this book is to examine the complex process that generates injunctions and to separate it into component parts, to be analyzed and then pieced back together. Along the way, it is sincerely hoped that the reader will grasp the very special character of this unique system of law that quests more for a fair and just result between the parties than for a comfortable pigeonholing of the problems that come before it.

Since this preface is being written after concluding work on the body of the text, I should like to express three enormous debts of gratitude for help, without which this book would never have come to pass: to my parents, for help and encouragement in more ways than I could ever begin to count; to my wife, for her inspiration, ideas and endless hours of work; and to Mary C. Carroll for her very real help through these months of production.

J. F. DOBBYN

December, 1973

OUTLINE

XIII

*

TABLE OF CASES

References are to Pages

TABLE OF CASES

TABLE OF CASES

XXI

TABLE OF CASES

TABLE OF CASES

TABLE OF CASES

INJUNCTIONS IN A NUTSHELL

CHAPTER I

GENERAL INTRODUCTION TO THE PROCESS OF DECISION IN ISSUING AN INJUNCTION

Perhaps the best place to insert the knife is right at the heart of the matter. The law of injunctions is different in *nature* from any other area of law; and it is the primary hope of the author to develop in the reader a sense of the peculiar nature of this form of relief, as well as an understanding of its common principles.

Since the heaviest ingredient in the decision to issue an injunction is the individual judge's discretion and sense of justice, no area of the law can lay truer claim to the characterization of "judge-made law." That being the case, the point of examination that will yield the clearest picture of what an injunction is all about is the decisional process of a judge in deciding whether an injunction is to issue. This process can best be understood by dividing it into three distinct stages. The kinds of decisions and degree of discretion employed by the court in each of these stages differ sharply from those employed in the other two stages.

A. STAGE ONE—JURISDICTION

The first stage involves the threshold question of power: does the court have *jurisdiction* over the parties and subject matter so as to vest it with the power to issue a valid injunction binding those whom it purports to bind? In this stage the court merely interprets and applies the law of jurisdiction without license of discretion.

B. STAGE TWO—EQUITY JURISDICTION

In the second stage, the court, having determined that as matter of power it *can* issue and enforce the injunction, decides the broad question of whether a court of equity *should* issue an injunction in the *type of case* before it. Here a particular kind of discretion enters the picture. Through the centuries, courts of equity have been led by considerations of logic and history to formulate, on a case by case basis, certain general principles of discretionary restraint on the full exercise of their power. These principles will be more fully discussed in Chapter III. By way of illustration, a court of equity will not grant an injunction when the petitioner has an adequate remedy at law or by way of self-help; a court of equity will not, except under certain conditions, interfere with the criminal law process by enjoining criminal conduct; a court of equity will not issue an injunction to aid a petitioner who is himself guilty of injustice in the matter before the court. In this second stage, the court is guided by these and other broad principles in determining whether or not an equity court *should* exercise or restrain its power to grant an injunction in this type of case. The court's "discretion" is limited by the guidance it receives from these evolved principles; but, on the other hand, by its decision in the case before it, the court takes part in moulding these broad policies of restraint. The somewhat misleading term applied to the area of potential judicial activity defined by these principles is "equity jurisdiction." The term is misleading because it does not refer to *power* (as is usually the case with the word "jurisdiction") but to *discretionary* policies concerning the proper role of a court of equity.

C. STAGE THREE—DISCRETION

In the third stage, the court focuses closely upon the particular facts of the case before it, analyzing and weighing the legitimate rights, interests, and concerns of the parties (with an eye also open to the public interest), and applies its *discretion* to achieve the result of maximum possible fairness and justice. In this third stage, the court employs a discretion vastly different from that employed in the second stage. Here the court's discretion is focused primarily on the relative rights and interests of the parties; there the major concern is the proper role of the equity court in the entire system of legal process. Here the court's discretion is bridled only by the limits of practicality in enforcing its injunction and by its concept of fairness and justice; there the court is merely sharing a small part in the discretion exercised by equity courts generally in drawing voluntary boundaries around their proper role and is therefore restrained by the already clearly evolved policies of restraint.

Just as it is easier to master a smooth golf swing by segregating and examining each of its elements in turn, it would be useful to do the same with the elements of each of the three stages of a decision to grant an injunction.

CHAPTER II

JURISDICTION

A. INTRODUCTION

Jurisdiction refers simply to the power of the court to decide the case before it. It must be considered in each of two aspects: power over the subject matter of the controversy, and power over the parties sought to be bound by the injunction. Problems of the ways in which a court obtains jurisdiction generally are dealt with in "Jurisdiction in a Nutshell." This volume will therefore deal with jurisdiction only as it relates peculiarly to a court's power to issue and enforce an injunction.

B. NATURE OF THE POWER OF THE EQUITY COURT

1. GENERALLY

The first essential step is to understand the exact nature of the power exercised by a court of equity in issuing injunctions. The spirit of it is caught in the cryptic phrase that equity courts have been incanting for centuries: "Equity acts in personam"—that is, "on the person." The key to the puzzle is to understand how literally that phrase is meant, and that can best be illustrated by an example. In Platt v. Woodruff, 61 N.Y. 378 (1875), a bank sued the petitioner at law on his personal note. The petitioner brought a separate bill in equity against the bank, alleging that the note was fraudulently obtained and seeking an injunction against further prosecution of the law suit by the bank. The injunction was issued; and subsequently, while the injunction was in force, the bank proceeded with the action at law and obtained a judgment against the petitioner. On appeal from that judgment, the question involved the effect of the injunction on the validity of the note, on the ability of the bank to obtain a judgment, and on the power of the law court to issue the judgment. In other words, did the injunction render the law judgment void? The court held that it did not, because of the purely personal nature of an injunction. Although the bank was ordered not to continue its law suit, it was not in any way deprived of its *power* to do so with full effect. Neither was the note itself in any way rendered void (principles of collateral estoppel and res judicata shall be discussed in a later chapter). *A fortiori*, the power of the law court to render a valid judgment on the note was unaffected by the injunction.

Then of what effect is an injunction? The key is that it acts strictly on the person of the party before the equity court. Its sole strength lies in the fact that if the bank chooses to disobey the injunction, the equity court can bring to bear the contempt sanctions of fine or imprisonment (where applicable) in order to penalize the bank punitively, to compel it to obey the order, or to compensate the petitioner for the violation. This is the total strength and effect of the injunction. In a case similar on the facts to Platt v. Woodruff, the court said, "the Chancery can do nothing but order him to prison, there to remain until he will obey. And this is all that court can do. And if the party will lie in prison rather than give up the obligation, the other is without remedy, and so the Chancellor has no power to nullify the obligation."

J.R. v. M.P., Ct. of Common Pleas 1459, 37 Henry 6, 13 Pl. 3 (1459).

This limitation causes large gaps in the court's ability to give any real effect to its injunctions. If an enjoined party manages to remove his person and property beyond the physical reaches of the court's territorial jurisdiction, he is beyond the court's power to compel obedience by the threat or imposition of sanctions. As shall be seen, courts in other jurisdictions will not aid the petitioner by enforcing per se the injunction obtained against the fleeing or out of state respondent.

With one exception to be discussed below, the court's ability to affect things as well as persons is limited to the scope of its physical power over them. For example, if the dispute concerns control of some physical thing such as machinery or a fund of money that is within the boundaries of the court's power acting through the sheriff, the court can grant relief to the petitioner, although the respondent is outside of the jurisdiction of the court (assuming, of course, that the requirements of due process are met). Pennington v. Fourth Nat. Bank, 243 U.S. 269 (1917); Geary v. Geary, 272 N.Y. 390, 6 N.E.2d 67 (1936). If, however, more than mere physical control is required to affect relief for the petitioner, as for example, to transfer legal title to land, the court of equity has no *inherent* power to go beyond the physical force it can exert on the person or thing. If, for example, the court wished to order specific performance of a contract to sell land within its jurisdiction, the court could force the defaulting seller himself to execute the necessary deed by the threat or imposition of contempt sanctions as long as the seller remained within the grasp of the court, and such a deed would be recognized as valid. If, however, the seller removed himsef and any leviable property beyond the court's reach, the court would have no *inherent* power to act to create or annul a deed on its own. Hart v. Sansom, 110 U.S. 151 (1884).

2. VESTING AND APPOINTIVE STATUTES

In order to cure this one particular problem of the court's impotence in the very sensitive area of titles to realty, most state legislatures have passed one of two types of statute granting an exceptional power to courts of equity. Under the first type of statute, if the court decrees that the respondent is to transfer title to the petitioner and the respondent refuses, the decree itself will operate to transfer title. This is the so-called "vesting statute". The second type of statute empowers the equity court to appoint a commissioner who would have authority to carry out the court decree to convey title on behalf of the defaulting seller. This is the so-called "appointive statute." With the limited exception of this extraordinary legislative grant of power to effect transfer of titles to realty, the actual force of any injunction is only that which the court can accomplish within its geographical jurisdiction by the threat or imposition of sanctions on the person enjoined or his property.

C. JURISDICTION OVER THE PERSON

A court of equity is vested with the power to issue a valid injunction only if it has jurisdiction in each of two senses: 1) jurisdiction over the *person* of those sought to be bound, and 2) jurisdiction over the *subject matter* of the cause of action. The word, "valid" in this context can most practically be defined to mean that if the injunction is violated by one sought to be bound by it, the violator can be subjected to the contempt process without thereby denying him due process under the Constitution. This seems to be the most appropriate focus because of the fact that the only practical strength of an injunction lies in the court's ability to enforce it through the exercise of physical sanctions of coercion or punishment of the violator and his property. (The limited effects of res judicata and collateral estoppel will be discussed later).

From this point of view, a consideration of jurisdiction over the person can be reduced to the question: Who, if anyone, can be held in contempt for violation of the injunction?

1. PARTIES

The class of "persons" who can potentially be bound by an injunction includes individuals, corporations, and any unincorporated association that has the legal status of being able to sue and be sued as an entity. Typical of this last category are labor unions and business partnerships.

The first, and most obvious group subject to the court's contempt powers for violation are those parties actually named in the injunction over whom the court has acquired personal jurisdiction in any of the ways outlined in "Jurisdiction in a Nutshell"—whether by personal service of process within the state or district, or by extraterritorial service under a long-arm statute, or by voluntary appearance in the equity action.

One traditional requirement of due process in regard to jurisdiction over parties is that they must have been given the opportunity to be heard directly or by representation at the hearing on issuance of the injunction. Baltz v. The Fair, 178 F.Supp. 691 (N.D.Ill.1959). A limited exception to this right to be heard has been carved out in the case of a temporary restraining order, where the emergency nature of the case demands immediate issuance of an injunction to prevent impending irreparable injury without time for notice and a hearing. (See, e. g., Rule 65b, Fed.Rules of Civ.Proc.) Such orders are strictly limited in scope and duration. (This topic will be discussed more fully below).

A second requirement is that the party to be held in contempt must have had actual knowledge of the injunction. Notice to the party can come from any source as long as it fulfills two requirements "first, it must proceed from a source entitled to credit; and second, it must inform the de-

[*11*]

fendant clearly and plainly from what act he must abstain." Cape May & Schellenger's Landing R. R. v. Johnson, 35 N.J.Eq. 422, 425 (Ch. 1882). In *Cape May*, for example, valid notice was sent by telegraph; and in United Packing House Workers v. Boynton, 240 Iowa 212, 35 N. W.2d 881 (1949), notice received by newspaper was sufficient.

2. PERSONS IN PRIVITY WITH A PARTY

The concept of "party" has been expanded by most courts to include any person in "privity" with a party—that is, "a person so identified in interest with a party as to represent the same legal rights and who is therefore bound by the judgment adjudging such rights. . . . Privity is not established merely because persons are interested in the same question or in proving the same set of facts or because the question litigated is one which might affect such other person's liability as a judicial precedent in a subsequent action." Baltz v. The Fair, 178 F.Supp. 691 (N.D. Ill.1959).

3. AIDERS AND ABETTORS

In order to prevent easy evasion of the effect of an injunction, a third group is added to those subject to the court's contempt powers. In the words of Learned Hand, "A person who knowingly assists a defendant in violating an injunction subjects himself to civil as well as criminal proceedings for contempt." Alemite Mfg. Corp. v. Staff, 42 F.2d 832 (2d Cir. 1930). By including this group, generally referred to as "aiders and abettors," the party is prevented from doing through another what he is enjoined from doing himself. To be bound, an aider and abettor must have actual knowledge of the injunction and purposefully act in the interest of an enjoined party in violation of the injunction. Merely accompanying a party or approving of the party's acts of violation is not sufficient. State v. Nouris, 15 Del.Ch. 282, 136 A. 887 (1927).

Since it is not merely the act that is enjoined, but the act *by a particular party,* if that party is not himself involved in the contempt, at least by way of collusive acquiescence, no action by a volunteer, even in the interests of the party, will subject the volunteer to contempt. It also follows that if the person sought to be held as an aider and abettor acts independently of the enjoined party solely for his own benefit, he is outside the reach of the injunction and cannot be held in contempt, even if the petitioner suffers the same type of harm as that sought to be prevented by the injunction. For example, in the *Alemite* case, supra, A was enjoined from violating the patent of Alemite. At the time, B was an employee of A

[*13*]

and was not named as a party in the action. Subsequently B left A's employment and set up a business of his own, in the course of which he infringed Alemite's patent. Alemite began proceedings to hold B in contempt. The second circuit ordered the contempt petition dismissed, holding, in the words of Learned Hand, that, "the only occasion when a person not a party may be punished, is when he has helped to bring about, not merely what the decree has forbidden, because it may have gone too far, but what it has power to forbid, an act of a party."

Often, tests similar to the general principles of agency are used to determine the status of an aider and abettor. For example, in the case of an employee, the party-employer need not have expressly authorized the particular act of his aider and abettor-employee as long as the employee acted within the scope of his authority in knowingly violating the injunction. (See Alemite Mfg. Corp. v. Staff, supra.) In ex parte Lennon, 166 U.S. 548 (1897), the employer-railroad was enjoined from refusing to accept cars of another railroad. The employee subsequently disobeyed the direction of the employer to accept such cars, and the employee was held in contempt since his act was found to be within the scope of his authority, and he had brought about that which was enjoined: the refusal by the railroad to accept the cars. If he had not been an employee, or

[14]

if his act had been outside the scope of his general duties for the employer, he could not have been held in contempt.   See Alemite Mfg. Corp. v. Staff, supra.

Since, by definition, an aider and abettor acts in the interest of a party, and that interest has been represented by the party at the hearing on issuance of the injunction, the aider and abettor is not allowed to reopen and litigate at the contempt hearing any of the issues underlying the original issuance of the injunction with the sole exception of lack of party or subject matter jurisdiction, which can be raised at any time.   He is, of course, allowed to argue by way of defense that he was not an aider and abettor, or that his acts did not constitute a violation of the injunction.

4. PERSONS IN SPECIAL RELATIONSHIP TO A RES

A further expansion of the group of persons bound by an injunction has been devised by equity courts in cases of injunctions which relate peculiarly to a particular property, business or office.   In such cases, if the injunction bound only the current holder of the office, or owner of the business or property, the effect of the injunction could be easily avoided by merely transferring the office, business or property to a successor in

[*15*]

interest. The entire procedure for the issuance of an injunction would have to be accomplished again with each change of personnel. In many cases the succession of personnel changes could stay one jump ahead of the petitioner continually.

To block this evasion, the equity courts have devised a theory whereby the injunction "attaches" to the particular "res"—the office, business or property concerned; and the injunction is thereafter binding on all who come into possession of the res with notice of the injunction. The concept resembles an "in rem" action; but the means of enforcing the injunction are still the familiar contempt sanctions against any violator.

a. SUCCESSORS IN OFFICE

In Crucia v. Behrman, 147 La. 144, 84 So. 525 (1920), the court enjoined Police Inspector Mooney from interfering with the petitioner in holding musical performances in his restaurant. Mooney was later succeeded in office by Police Inspector Boyle, who arrested the petitioner for the acts mentioned in the injunction. Boyle was neither named in the injunction nor connected with the police force at the time of its issuance, although he was aware of its existence. The court held that, "In such cases the [injunction] runs against the office, and embraces all who are charged with the execution of its functions and the official acts sought to be prohibited, whether by the present incumbent or others who may succeed to such duties; and they are guilty of contempt if they have knowledge of the existence of such [injunction]."

The same rule of extension has been applied to successors in private as well as public office, such as presidents and directors of corporations, and trustees, as long as the successor acted with knowledge of the injunction.

Fed. must be in concert

(i) The Federal Rule

The federal courts are under a special restriction in respect to successors in office because of Rule 65(d), of the Federal Rules of Civil Procedure, which states that every federal injunction *Actual Notice* "is binding only upon the parties to the action, their officers, agents, servants, employees, and attorneys, and upon those persons in active concert or participation with them who receive actual notice of the order by personal service or otherwise." This language was strictly interpreted by Justice Jackson in Regal Knitwear Co. v. NLRB, 324 U.S. 9 (1945):

> "The term 'successors and assigns' in an enforcement order of course may not enlarge its scope beyond that defined by the Federal Rules of Civil Procedure. Successors and assigns may, however, be instrumentalities through which defendant seeks to evade an

> order or may come within the description of
> persons in active concert or participation
> with them in the violation of an injunction.
> If they are, by that fact they are brought
> within scope of contempt proceedings by the
> rules of civil procedure."

Under this interpretation, successors or assigns
could only be bound if they also qualified as aiders and abettors. Nevertheless, in the 1963 case
of Lucy v. Adams, 224 F.Supp. 79 (N.D.Ala.
1963), the reach of an injunction against discrimination on the basis of race was extended to the
successor in office of the Dean of Admissions of
the University of Alabama where there was no
evidence of collusion or agency between the enjoined dean and his successor. The court felt authorized to make this exception to Rule 65(d) because of Rule 25(d) which provides generally for
the substitution of the successor of a *public* office
holder as a party in an action. But the court
drew major support for its decision to exercise its
authority from state case law such as Crucia v.
Behrman, discussed above. The cases of Wright
v. County School Board of Greenville Co., Va.,
309 F.Supp. 671 (E.D.Va.1970) (municipal body
succeeding to the school supervising powers of
the enjoining body held bound by the injunction)
and Lankford v. Gelston, 364 F.2d 197 (4th Cir.
1966) (successor to enjoined police commissioner

bound) have continued the line of cases following
Lucy v. Adams.

Assignee included

b. ASSIGNEE OF A BUSINESS

In Sperry & Hutchinson Co. v. McKelvey
Hughes Co., 64 Pa.Super. 57 (1916) the equity
court enjoined the respondent, McKelvey Hughes
Company, from engaging in certain unfair business practices toward petitioner's customers.
Shortly after the decree was issued some of the
persons connected with the respondent formed a
new corporation to avoid the effects of the decree. The new corporation, which conducted its
business affairs contrary to the dictates of the injunction, was acting in the interest of its own
members, and not as aider and abettor of the
original corporation, the only party to the injunction proceeding. Nevertheless, to prevent the
complete sidestepping of the injunction, the court
held the new corporation in contempt. Case law
in this area is scant, but what little exists indicates that as a general rule, if the assignment of
a business is accomplished for the purpose of
evading the effect of an injunction, the assignee
can be held bound.

c. SUCCESSOR IN INTEREST IN PROPERTY

The most common extension of the reach of an
injunction beyond parties and aiders and abettors

occurs in cases where specific property, real or personal, is being used in such a way as to create a nuisance. The court can issue an injunction "ad rem", that is, against the property itself, enjoining the unlawful use of the property by anyone. The injunction is said to "attach" to the property and binds anyone with notice of the injunction. In the case of personal property, actual knowledge of the injunction is a requisite for contempt. Where the injunction runs against a particular use of real property, however, so that the injunction can be recorded with the title to the property, any person acquiring an interest in the realty as owner or lessee is considered to have constructive notice sufficient to be bound by the injunction. All others are not bound unless they have actual knowledge of the injunction, as in the case of personalty. For example, in State v. Terry, 99 Wash. 1, 168 P. 513 (1917), the court declared a particular building used for prostitution a nuisance and enjoined the owners and "all other persons whatsoever" from using the building for purposes of prostitution. Terry was not a party to the action and was not served with a copy of the injunction. She was, however, a lessee and was therefore under constructive notice of the injunction and could be held in contempt for its violation.

There is no set formulation of words whereby an injunction is transformed into one attaching to

the property. The court in *Terry* stated that if
the decree is broad enough in its terms to purport
to enjoin *all persons*, it is sufficient notice that
the injunction is intended to attach to the property.

Here again, the reach of federal injunctions is
limited by Rule 65(d) to parties, their officers,
agents, servants, employees, attorneys and those
persons in active concert or participation with
them who receive actual notice of the order.
This precludes extending an "ad rem" injunction
to any person merely dealing with the property
with knowledge of the injunction as was done in
the *Terry* case. See United States v. Dean Rubber Mfg. Co., 71 F.Supp. 96 (W.D.Mo.1946).

5. QUASI IN REM JURISDICTION

One final category of persons bound by an injunction has been created by an approach peculiar to the equity courts of New Jersey. In Wil-
entz v. Edwards, 134 N.J.Eq. 522, 36 A.2d 423
(1944), the Attorney General began an investiga-
tion into the activities of certain securities dealers to see if the state's Blue Sky Law was being
violated. The dealers were then located outside
of New Jersey, and therefore no personal jurisdiction could be obtained over them. On application of the Attorney General, the state court of
equity issued an order to the effect that the out-

of-state dealers were to appear and testify before the Attorney General and produce books and papers as required; and that until they did so, these dealers were enjoined from purchasing or selling securities within the state. The respondent-dealers, having been notified of the injunction, raised the issue of its validity in the absence of personal jurisdiction over them. The court held the injunction valid on a *quasi in rem* theory. In essence, since the state has the right to prohibit the sale of securities except by license, it can condition the granting of such license on the respondent's complying with the order to provide relevant information. The state does not deprive the respondent of any right by this injunction; it merely withholds a *privilege* until the respondent complies with a reasonable condition.

As stated, this theory is a limited one. It would seem to allow an injunction to issue against an out-of-state respondent upon mere notice when, 1) the bill is filed in the public interest by the state Attorney General, 2) seeking an injunction against activity which the state has a right under its police power to prohibit except by license, and 3) the specific injunction is a reasonable step in execution of that licensing power.

This theory has not been adopted outside of New Jersey; and with the increase of methods for obtaining personal jurisdiction over out-of-state respondents, such as long-arm statutes (see

"Jurisdiction in a Nutshell"), it is unlikely that other states will find it necessary to resort to this kind of conceptualism.

6. PERSONS NOT BOUND BY INJUNCTION

The converse of the proposition that an injunction is binding on parties, those in privity with parties, aiders and abettors of parties, certain assignees and successors, and those with proper notice dealing with property to which an injunction has attached, is that all other persons are not bound by the injunction, and it is beyond the power of the court to hold them in contempt for its violation. A court of equity "cannot lawfully enjoin the world at large, no matter how broadly it words its decree. If it assumes to do so, the decree is pro tanto brutum fulmen [to that extent, sound and fury, signifying nothing], and the persons enjoined are free to ignore it." Alemite Mfg. Corp. v. Staff, supra.

D. JURISDICTION OVER THE SUBJECT MATTER

The second aspect of jurisdiction necessary to empower the court to issue a valid injunction is jurisdiction over the subject matter of the action. This can best be understood by considering it from the point of view of the *limitations* on the court's subject matter jurisdiction.   There are two primary areas of limitation to consider; 1) restrictions on the kind of action that can be heard by an equity court; and 2) restrictions on the kind of relief that can be granted.   In the following discussion of these restrictions, the key point to keep in mind is that each is a limitation on the power of the court to act at all.

a.   RESTRICTIONS ON ALL EQUITY COURTS

1.   *Restrictions on Kinds of Actions*

The evolution of the areas in which equity courts are empowered to administer relief has been more a function of history than of planning. In the development of the current court system from its English predecessor, certain types of courts were allotted exclusive jurisdiction over certain types of disputes to the exclusion of all other courts.   For example, it is a universal rule that only courts of law are empowered to try criminal cases.   (The subject of criminal contempt will be discussed below).   It is also typical of state court systems that separate specialized courts have been granted exclusive jurisdiction over divorce and other family matters, as well as matters of probate.   These divisions of authority have almost universally been crystalized by stat-

[24]

ute, so that no question exists but that a court of equity does not have the power to hear and adjudicate a criminal case, or one involving divorce or the probate of a will.

b. RESTRICTIONS ON CERTAIN EQUITY COURTS

In certain areas in which it has been considered essential to have only federal courts interpreting and applying federal law, such as the area covered by the Securities and Exchange Act of 1934, federal statutes have vested exclusive jurisdiction in the federal courts, thereby removing the power of any state equity court to hear an action arising under that Act.   See Securities Exchange Act of 1934, § 27.

Federal courts are themselves limited as to subject matter jurisdiction, first and foremost by Article III, Section 2 of the United States Constitution which grants, and thereby circumscribes, the authority of federal courts to hear cases.   A further Constitutional limitation is found in the Eleventh Amendment:

> "The Judicial power of the United States shall not be construed to extend to any suit in law or equity, commenced or prosecuted against one of the United States by Citizens of another State, or by Citizens or Subjects of any Foreign State."

The distinct contours of the two commonly applied doctrines of "federal question" and "diversity of citizenship" jurisdiction have been worked out in federal decisional law.

Congress has also, from time to time, enacted statutes limiting or dividing federal court jurisdiction over various types of cases. For example, under section 204(d) of the Emergency Price Control Act of 1942, exclusive jurisdiction to enjoin enforcement of any section of the Act or regulation thereunder was vested in the Emergency Court of Appeals and the Supreme Court on review, to the exclusion of all other federal as well as state courts.

2. RESTRICTIONS ON KINDS OF RELIEF THAT MAY BE GRANTED

The second type of limitation commonly placed upon subject matter jurisdiction is a restriction on the kind of *relief* that may be granted. This restriction can be either inherent or statutory. For example, it is inherently beyond the power of a court of equity to create or annul a deed or other legal instrument absent some special statutory grant of power such as occurs in a "vesting" type of statute (as discussed above.) The court's power to enforce an injunction, and therefore make it meaningful, is also inherently limited by the geographical boundaries of its physical power (acting through the sheriff or commissioners) over the person or property of the respondent. Although *res judicata* effect is given to findings of fact underlying a decree, the actual injunctive order of one court of equity is not entitled to full faith and credit by any other court. (See discussion on Extraterritorial Effect, below). This creates a severe practical geographical limit on the power of the court to issue an enforceable injunction.

Equity courts are also under numerous statutory restrictions on the relief they can grant. For example, in an effort to preserve the balance between state and federal powers essential to our system of federalism, 28 U.S.C.A. § 2283 was enacted to provide that, "A court of the United States may not grant an injunction to stay proceedings in a State court except as expressly authorized by Act of Congress, or where necessary in aid of its jurisdiction, or to protect or effectuate its judgments." In other words, unless the subject matter of the particular case fits within one of the three exceptions stated in the statute, once an action has begun in a state court, no federal court can enjoin continuance of the prosecution of that action to its conclusion.

Another example is found in Section 4 of the Norris-LaGuardia Act, 29 U.S.C.A. § 104. In order to put an end to "midnight injunctions" as a weapon of management at a time when it was thought that labor needed assistance to help equalize bargaining positions, Congress passed an act severely limiting the power of federal courts to enjoin strikes and other labor union activity.

Particular limitations on injunctions in specific fields such as labor relations exist at both the state and federal level. They occur generally in areas in which the legislative body feels that a group or industry is in need of special protection from the existing functioning of the equity process.

E. COMPARISON OF JURISDICTION OVER THE PERSON WITH JURISDICTION OVER THE SUBJECT MATTER

The major characteristic in common between these two elements of jurisdiction is that a lack of either will render the equity court impotent to issue a valid injunction in the case before it.

One difference between the two is that if the defect is in jurisdiction over a particular party, the equity court could, in a given case, issue an injunction valid as to those parties over whom it has personal jurisdiction and invalid as to those over whom it does not. The injunction could be disobeyed with impugnity by the latter (unless a doctrine such as aider and abettor applied) but would be binding on the former. If the defect is in subject matter jurisdiction, however, any injunction would be altogether void as to all parties.

It should also be noted that a respondent, physically beyond the reach of the court for purposes of personal jurisdiction, can voluntarily enter a general appearance and thereby confer personal jurisdiction on the court. By comparison, it is beyond the power of the parties to the action by agreement or estoppel to confer subject matter jurisdiction on the court when it has been denied to the court by an inherent, statutory or constitutional limitation, such as those discussed above.

Another difference lies in this: if a case comes before an equity court which presents a substantial question as to whether or not the court has subject matter jurisdiction, the court has inherent power to issue a temporary injunction to hold the *status quo* between the parties to give the court a reasonable time within which to decide whether or not it has subject matter jurisdiction. If this injunction is violated, the court can validly impose criminal contempt sanctions to vindicate the authority of the court even though it is ultimately determined that the court does not have subject matter jurisdiction in the action. In the case of United States v. United Mine Workers, 330 U.S. 258 (1947), for example, the United States brought suit against the union, seeking 1)

[29]

[handwritten: S. M. Jurisdiction. Even if void, must follow injunction.]

[handwritten: Personal Jurisdiction, May be ignored]

a judgment that the union had no power to termi-
nate a collective bargaining agreement unilateral-
ly, and 2) an injunction against a threatened
strike by the union. The court, *ex parte,* issued a
temporary restraining order against the union's
planned strike. The union chose to disobey the
injunction in the belief that Section 4 of the Norris-LaGuardia Act removed the court's power to
issue the injunction. The union was held in contempt; and, on appeal, the Supreme Court sustained the contempt sanctions imposed punitively
to vindicate the authority of the court, thereby
upholding the district court's power to hold the
status quo pending its decision of a substantial
threshold question of subject matter jurisdiction,
regardless of the outcome on that issue. It was
noted that if this claim of jurisdiction had been
"frivolous and not substantial", the contempt decree would not have been sustained.

By comparison, no such exception exists to allow the court to hold the *status quo* while it tries
out threshold issues of *personal* jurisdiction.
Any injunction issued without jurisdiction over a
party is void as to that party and can be disobeyed with impugnity.

F. STANDING TO RAISE THE ISSUE OF LACK OF JURISDICTION

Any injunction issued by a court without jurisdiction—that is, without the power to do so, is inherently void. For this reason, lack of jurisdiction can be called to the attention of the court at any time, by any of the parties or by the court itself on its own motion. Once the court is aware of the lack of jurisdiction, it can take steps to declare what is already the fact, namely, that the injunction is void. This is generally accomplished by an order formally vacating the injunction.

Can be raised at any time

It also follows that since an injunction issued without jurisdiction is void, there is no time limitation on raising the issue by any party or the court. If, for example, the defect is not called to the attention of the court until after final judgment, or even after time for appeal has expired, the voidness of the decree is not cured, and no party is estopped or precluded from having it then vacated or defending against the imposition of contempt sanctions on this ground.

Similarly, one being charged with violating the order as an aider and abettor, or successor in interest, can attack the validity of the order itself on this limited ground of lack of jurisdiction.

CHAPTER III

EQUITY JURISDICTION

A. DEFINITION

Assuming that the court has jurisdiction over the parties and subject matter in a particular case so that a valid injunction *can* be issued, the second step is to decide as a matter of discretionary self-regulation whether or not it would be appropriate to the proper role of the court of equity to grant an injunction in this type of case. This is the meaning of equity jurisdiction. The delineation of the "proper role" of the court of equity is contained in a body of general principles, developed by the court on a case by case basis. The equity court has, in essence, defined its own function, guided by historical and political considerations (as in the case of the principle that equity will not act if the petitioner has an adequate remedy at law) as well as by concern for its own image (an equity court will not issue a decree that it cannot enforce), and considerations of fairness (equity will not aid a petitioner who is himself guilty of injustice in the matter before the court).

The unfortunate choice of the phrase "equity jurisdiction", with its connotations of power rather than discretion, together with the imprecise use of words such as "can" rather than "should" in some court opinions, has had the tendency to blur the important distinction between power and discretion. Several important consequences flow from this distinction that have serious practical implications for the parties to an action. For example, an injunction issued without jurisdiction is void, and can be disobeyed with impugnity. An injunction issued contrary to the principles of equity jurisdiction, however, is simply erroneous, and is in full effect as to the parties until it is vacated. If, for example, the court were to issue an injunction erroneously in a case in which the petitioner had a completely adequate remedy at law, the respondent would nevertheless be bound by the injunction, and would be liable to contempt for its violation.

A second major distinction is that the issue of lack of equity jurisdiction is deemed waived if not raised by the respondent by way of demurrer or answer. Once waived, lack of equity jurisdiction cannot thereafter be raised by the respondent by way of defense, appeal, or collateral attack.

If the issue is raised at the appropriate time by the respondent, and the court erroneously rules in favor of the petitioner, the respondent's only recourse is by way of appeal. If the lower court is erroneously affirmed on appeal, the matter is at an end. In no event can the injunction be attacked collaterally or at the time of a contempt hearing on the grounds of lack of equity jurisdiction.

By contrast, lack of jurisdiction cannot be waived by the parties so as to vest the court with power to issue a valid injunction. It can be raised by any party or the court itself, before, during, or after issuance of the injunction, by direct appeal or by collateral attack.

B. PRINCIPLES

With this general background on equitable jurisdiction, the next step is to consider the principles that give it form.

No jury system.

1. ADEQUATE REMEDY AT LAW

The principle that equity will not grant relief to a petitioner who has an adequate remedy at law is a product of the political pressures that surrounded the equity court in England during the early days of its formation and development. Equitable relief was originally obtained through the Chancellor as a special exercise of the king's perogative to administer justice to his subjects as a matter of grace. Once the "caseload" of the Chancellor rose to such proportions that an entirely separate system of courts, parallel to the common law courts, was needed, the jealousy of those involved in the established common law court system created pressures that compelled the equity system to retrench behind barriers that would prevent unnecessary encroachment on the jurisdiction of the common law courts. Since the Chancellor granted equitable relief as a matter of discretion rather than right, the safest method of avoiding a direct collision course between the two court systems, that could have led to the abolition of the less established equity system, was to confine the granting of relief to that class of cases in which the ordinary processes of the common law were inadequate to do justice to the petitioner. This also comported with the Aristotelian concept of "equity" as a *rectification* of the ineffectiveness of the law to produce justice in a particular case because of its necessary generality. Consistent observance of this restraint has crystalized it into the established principle that equity will act only where there is no adequate remedy at law.

Justification for retaining the principle today, particularly in jurisdictions where law and equity are merged into one court system (as under the federal rules of civil procedure), lies primarily in the fact that the respondent has no right to a trial by jury in an equity action. This was the case with the English legal system at the time of its adoption in this country, and the constitutional grant of the right to a jury trial in civil cases has always been interpreted to imply an exception for cases properly brought in equity. If the traditional area of operation of equity courts were enlarged by simply eliminating or curtailing the principle that equity will not act where there is an adequate legal remedy, there would be a concomitant erosion of this constitutional right to a jury trial.

Another consideration occasionally referred to by commentators is that injunctions are more difficult and cumbersome to enforce than simple money judgments; and therefore, in cases where the legal remedy is at least as efficient as the equitable remedy, there is no reason in theory not to stick to the simpler of the two.

The catalogue of remedies that an equity court will consider in deciding whether the petitioner has adequate relief elsewhere is as follows: 1) *Money damages* in an action at law; 2) *detinue* for recovery of personal property from one who acquired it lawfully but retains it without right; 3) *replevin* for recovery of personal property taken unlawfully; 4) *Extraordinary legal remedies* (e. g. in Harvey v. Kirton, 182 Iowa 973, 164 N.W. 888 (1917), the petitioner asked the court to enjoin the directors and officers of a newly formed school district from performing the duties of the office on the grounds that the school district had been created unlawfully. The court dismissed the petition because the petitioner had an adequate legal remedy by way of *quo warranto* to test the legitimacy of this quasi-corporation); 5) *Crimi-*

[*36*]

nal sanctions available where the activity sought to be enjoined violates the criminal law (this subject will be more fully explored below in the discussion of the principle that equity will not enjoin a criminal act); 6) *Administrative procedures* (In Myers v. Bethlehem Shipbuilding Corp., 303 U.S. 41 (1938), petitioner sought an injunction against an NLRB hearing on the question of an unfair labor practice. The Supreme Court denied the injunction on several grounds, one of which was the principle, "frequently applied in equity where relief by injunction was sought," that administrative remedies must be exhausted before injunctive relief can be sought); 7) *Political processes* (In Winnett v. Adams, 71 Neb. 817, 99 N. W. 681 (1904), the petitioners sought to enjoin the Republican county central committee from enforcing committee rules which would prevent them from fairly submitting lists of delegates to the voters in a primary election. The court held that the petitioner must look to the political process for protection of his political rights and sustained the demurrer. See also, O'Brien v. Brown, 409 U.S. 1 (1972), wherein the Supreme Court expressed reluctance to interfere by injunction in the matter of unseating delegates to the Democratic National Convention.); 8) *Police or self-help* (In Mechanics Foundry v. Ryall, 75 Cal. 601 17 P. 703 (1888), the petitioner asked the court to enjoin an employee who had been dismissed from returning each day and occupying his former work bench. The court refused relief on the ground that the petitioner had an adequate remedy by way of self-help in simply refusing admittance to the respondent, or by way of calling for police assistance in removing him from the premises.).

Case law has given rise to a number of formulas for the measurement of the adequacy of legal relief. For example, in Boyce v. Grundy, 28 U.S. 210 (1830), the Supreme Court said, "It is not enough that there is a remedy at law; it must be plain and adequate, or in other words, as practical and as efficient to the ends of justice and its prompt administration, as the remedy in equity." The key words in this often-quoted formula seem to be "practical," "efficient," and "prompt". Inadequacy will be found if the legal remedy cannot prevent or repair the injury to petitioner's rights as effectively as injunctive relief, if it is appreciably more cumbersome procedurally, or if it will entail a significantly greater delay in producing relief.

While inadequacy of remedy can take innumerable forms, the most common categories are the following.

a. PROTECTION OF INTEREST IN LAND

Because of the economic, social and political importance attached to land in England at the time this principle was being established, the courts created a conclusive presumption that no measure of money damages would be as effective a remedy as one that would restore or preserve an interest in land. For this reason, unless an action of ejectment at law, or some equivalent statutory relief, is available, the court will not allow the availability of money damages to stand in the way of ordering specific performance of a contract for the transfer of an interest in land, or enjoining damage to land, or interference with its rightful enjoyment. If a threatened trespass involves the removal of any part of the realty, such as the carrying away of coal or ore or earth, it makes no difference that the thing carried away is of relatively low value. If it is a part of the estate in land that is being destroyed or removed, money damages will not be considered adequate. Richards v. Dower, 64 Cal. 62, 28 P. 113 (1883).

Similarly, if the trespass poses the threat of ripening into an easement, it is conclusively presumed that the damage remedy is inadequate. This was the case in Richards v. Dower, supra, where the respondent was erecting a permanent tunnel for a distance of 15 feet under the petitioner's lot.

One precaution should be noted. It was an ancient doctrine that equity would not determine a controversy involving the *legal* title to land. That rule survives in this altered form. If the respondent in an injunction action genuinely disputes ownership of *legal* title to the land, either party has the right to have that issue tried to a jury in a court of law. The party claiming the right must demand it in his pleadings, or he will be considered to have waived it. The usual procedure is for the equity court to grant a preliminary injunction to hold the *status quo* between the parties until the issue of legal title can be tried out at law. If the petitioner fails to institute the action at law, or the decision of the law court is adverse to the petitioner, the preliminary injunction is vacated and the equity action is dismissed. If the petitioner is successful at law, the equity court will then proceed to the merits of the action for a permanent injunction. See Moore v. McAllister, 216 Md. 497, 141 A.2d 176 (1958).

b. PROTECTION OF INTERESTS IN UNIQUE PERSONAL PROPERTY

The remedy of money damages in cases involving personal property will be considered inadequate only if the property is somehow unique and irreplaceable. This occurs most commonly with art objects, deeds of title, or objects such as gifts or heirlooms to which sentimental value has been attached. The test in the latter case is not merely the subjective attachment of the petitioner to the object, but the objective test of whether a reasonable person would form a sentimental attachment to the object under the circumstances.

There are also cases in which the object itself is not unique or irreplaceable, but circumstances render it of extraordinary importance to the petitioner. In McGowin v. Remington, 12 Pa. 56 (1849), for example, the petitioner sought recovery *in specie* of documents and instruments necessary to his trade as a surveyor. Although most of the materials could, in time, have been replaced, they were of immediate need to the petitioner in carrying on his business, and the loss of profits for the period of time he would be without them would not be susceptible of measurement. Therefore the court held that legal relief by way of money damages was not an adequate remedy.

The second type of case in which non-unique goods are considered proper subjects for equitable relief is one in which the uncertainty of the future plays a role. Buxton v. Lister, 3 Atk. 384 (1748), involved a petition for specific enforcement of an agreement for the purchase of several parcels of growing wood, to be cut and paid for over a period of eight years. The court granted equitable relief, noting the distinction between a contract for immediate performance and one to be performed over the course of years. Where the objects are not unique, the former case lends itself to simple legal relief by way of money damages; but the latter case involves more than the mere transfer of presently replaceable objects. It involves security against the uncertainty of future years in regard to the price and availability of the subject of the contract, and this added element is not susceptible of accurate valuation.

c. VIOLATION OF CONFIDENTIAL RELATIONS

Equity courts have traditionally filled the gap left by courts of law in the protection of relationships of trust and confidence, particularly in a business context. While the inability to fix accurate money damages might arguably be sufficient to make the injury irreparable in most of these cases, equity courts are inclined to give the most serious consideration to a petitioner's claim that the respondent is injuring his business, or taking an unfair advantage, by abusing a confidence reasonably placed in him. For example, in Herold v. Herold China & Pottery Co., 257 F. 911 (6th Cir.1919), the court stated:

> "The rule is well settled that secret formulas and processes, such as are claimed to be

involved here, are property rights which will be protected by injunction, not only as against those who attempt to disclose or use them in violation of confidential relations or contracts express or implied, but as against those who are participating in such attempt with knowledge of such confidential relations or contract, though they might in time have reached the same result by their own independent experiments or efforts."

d. DAMAGES DIFFICULT TO MEASURE

It frequently happens that the inadequacy of legal relief stems from the difficulty of fixing the dollar value of the injury to the rights or property of the petitioner. One typical area is the loss of business income. In Justices v. Griffin Road Co., 11 Ga. 246 (1852), for example, injunctive relief was granted to prevent interference with petitioner's toll-gate. The legal remedy of money damages was considered inadequate because of the difficulty of proving how much revenue from the toll road would be lost over any given period of time.

Another such area involves injury to intangible rights. In Strank v. Mercy Hospital of Johnston, 383 Pa. 54, 117 A.2d 697 (1955), for example, petitioner sought a court order compelling respondent to give her transfer credits for two years of study as a student nurse, completed before her dismissal in the third year for violation of a rule of the school. The court overruled respondent's preliminary objections which were based on the claim of adequate remedy at law, holding that, "it is the peculiar province of equity to afford relief where the measurement of damages in such cases cannot be formulated and applied in a suit at law because of their being necessarily speculative and indeterminate, and therefore the legal remedy is not adequate and complete."

A third such area involves cases wherein the crux of the harm lies in its affect on the sensibilities of the petitioner personally. In Mooney v. Cooledge, 30 Ark. 640 (1875), both petitioners and respondents claimed title to an acre of ground that had been used by petitioner's ancestors as a family burial ground. Petitioners sought to enjoin respondents from removing the remains of their relatives and friends from that area in order to convert it to a roadway. The court held that, "The extent of the injury to be inflicted must depend upon the sympathies and feelings of the parties injured, and their peculiar views as to the sacredness of the spot where the remains rest. Whilst it might be a matter of little moment to some, it might inflict an irreparable injury to others, which money could not compensate."

[44]

e. MULTIPLE ACTIONS AT LAW REQUIRED

A fourth common instance of inadequacy of legal remedy is the type of case in which numerous law suits would be required to accomplish what equity could do in one action. For example, in Colliton v. Oxborough, 86 Minn. 361, 90 N.W. 793 (1902), the respondent claimed to have leased farmland from the petitioner and threatened to enter upon the petitioner's land, put in crops, harvest them, and prevent the petitioner or anyone else from cultivating the land. The court found that no lease had been executed and granted an injunction against respondent's threatened trespasses, stating, "if a threatened trespass to real property consists of a single act, which will be temporary in its effect, a court of equity, if the wrongdoer be solvent, will not interfere, but leave the injured party to his action at law for damages. But if the trespass is continuous in its nature, and its repetition is threatened, equity, although each act of treaspass, if taken by itself, would not be destructive of the freehold, and the legal remedy would be adequate if each act stood alone, will prevent the threatened wrong by injunction, because the injured party has not a complete and adequate remedy by one action at law for the entire wrong, while a court of equity, by preventing the wrong, affords in a single action a complete remedy."

f. IMPRACTICAL REMEDY AT LAW

A fifth category consists of instances in which a legal remedy exists in theory, but for some reason cannot produce the practical result of actual relief to the petitioner. Two examples are the following.

(i) *Insolvency of Respondent*

It is frequently the case that, in theory, money damages would adequately compensate petitioner for his injury; but that, practically speaking, no legal judgment would result in cash in the hands of the petitioner because of the insolvency of the respondent. There are three different approaches taken by courts to the question of whether or not respondent's insolvency amounts to inadequacy of legal remedy. The majority and sounder view follows the tradition of equity in looking through form to substance, and holds that any remedy that cannot result in actual relief to the petitioner because of the respondent's insolvency is inadequate. See, e. g., Gause v. Perkins, 3 Jones Eq. 177, 69 Am.Dec. 728, (North Carolina 1857). In granting equitable relief in this type of case, however, equity courts will exercise caution to avoid giving an unjust preference to the petitioner over the respondent's other creditors.

In McNamara v. Home Land & Cattle Co., 105 F. 202 (C.C.Mont.1900), reversed on other grounds, 111 F. 822, the court went one step further in holding that the legal remedy against a solvent out-of-state corporation was inadequate because the corporation had no reachable assets within the state of Montana, and could therefore be treated "as if insolvent in Montana."

The second clear-cut approach is that of Pennsylvania and a minority of jurisdictions:

> "The fact, if it be so, that this remedy may not be successful in realizing the fruits of a recovery at law, on account of the insolvency of the defendants, is not of itself a ground of equitable interference. The remedy is what is to be looked at. If it exist, and is ordinarily adequate, its possible want of success is not a consideration." Heilman v. The Union Canal Co., 37 Pa.St. 100 (1860).

Although these jurisdictions are adamant in holding that insolvency is never a sufficient reason of itself to hold the legal remedy inadequate, they frequently cite insolvency as a makeweight consideration to be taken into account with other factors.

The third approach is that adopted by West Virginia in holding that respondent's insolvency

renders legal relief inadequate in actions of trespass or nuisance, Marcum v. Marcum, 57 W.Va.
285, 50 S.E. 246 (1905), but not in contract actions for specific performance. George E. Warren Co. v. A. L. Black Coal Co., 85 W.Va. 684,
102 S.E. 672 (1920). No clear reason is given for
the distinction between the two kinds of action.

(ii) *Serious Risks Involved in Executing Legal Relief*

Occasionally the situation will arise in which
the execution of the available legal remedy will
involve serious risk of loss to the petitioner or
the sheriff. For example, in Hirschberg v. Flus-
ser, 87 N.J.Eq. 588, 101 A. 191 (1917), the respondent intended to erect a building. He excavated to a depth of 24 feet, and in doing so, he
excavated a portion of petitioner's adjoining
property. He then built a foundation and side
wall up to ground level on his own land and also
on that of the petitioner. The petitioner brought,
and won, a legal action of ejectment, but found
that the sheriff refused to execute the judgment
without indemnification by the petitioner because
the wall had been constructed of stones so large
that they extended from the petitioner's property
onto the respondent's property, and it would have
been impossible to remove the encroaching part
without injuring the part of the wall resting on
the respondent's land. The petitioner's subse-

quent bill for an injunction, placing the responsibility for removing the encroaching part of the wall on the respondent, was granted. The court held that a legal remedy that involved serious risk of injury to the respondent's property, for which the petitioner or the sheriff would have been liable, was inadequate.

This rule is commonly followed in cases of construction that overlaps onto a petitioner's property.

g. INJURY CAUSED BY ABUSE OF COURT PROCESS

Perhaps the epitome of the lack of adequate remedy at law exists in the unusual case in which the injury of which the petitioner complains is *caused*, or about to be caused, by an abuse of the legal process itself by the respondent. In such a case, depending upon a number of factors, the court will frequently enjoin the respondent from commencing or continuing the offending legal action.

(i) *Injunction Against Criminal Prosecution— Injury to Personal Rights*

One historic case that touched off an avalanche of requests for injunctions against criminal prosecutions, mainly because of the ambiguity of the opinion, was Dombrowski v. Pfister, 380 U.S. 479

(1965). The petitioner was an organization that was active in promoting civil rights for black citizens in Louisiana. It asked the federal court to enjoin the governor, police, and law enforcement officials of the state from prosecuting its members for alleged violations of the Louisiana Subversive Activities and Communist Control Law and the Communist Propaganda Control Law. While the criminal trial and appellate process are usually presumed adequate protection for any related constitutional rights of defendants, the petitioner argued that 1) the criminal statutes under which the prosecutions were brought were constitutionally void for vagueness; and 2) arrests and searches were made, and prosecutions were threatened, with no real expectation of convictions, but merely for the bad faith purpose of harassing the organization's members and discouraging them from continuing their civil rights activities. Since indictments could be dismissed or prosecutions terminated in a number of ways that would never produce a conclusory finding on the statute's unconstitutionality, thereby leaving the authorities free to continue a plan of harassment with its intended "chilling effect" on petitioner's first amendment freedoms of speech and assembly, no real protection for these important freedoms could be found in the usual criminal process. The Supreme Court was sufficiently convinced of the seriousness of this irreparable harm

Dombrowski ① Bad faith prosecution (no opp. to defend property)
② Invalid unconstitutional statute,
③ Chilling effect in (1st Amendment)
PRINCIPLES   Ch. 3

and lack of any adequate legal remedy to overcome two major stumbling blocks to injunctive
relief—1) the reluctance to interfere with any-
thing as critical to the public welfare as enforcement of the criminal law, and 2) the spirit of federalism which proscribes unwarranted federal in-
tervention in state affairs.   The injunction was
therefore issued.   An unfortunate ambiguity in
the opinion left open the serious question of just
what elements a petitioner would have to establish in order to have a federal court enjoin criminal prosecutions under a state law.   Was it necessary to prove a case substantially similar to the
situation of *Dombrowski,* including the element
of threats of prosecution in *bad faith* for the purpose of chilling the exercise of first amendment
rights;   or was it sufficient to show merely that
prosecution was about to be brought under an unconstitutional criminal statute with the *effective
result* of chilling first amendment freedoms?   It
was impossible to tell how the Supreme Court
would rule on that precise question because it
was not an issue in *Dombrowski.*   After considerable confusion among the lower courts, the Supreme Court decided in Younger v. Harris, 401
U.S. 37 (1971), that the policies of federalism and
non-interference in criminal law enforcement
could not be overcome by a showing of less than
bad faith enforcement, or threat of enforcement,
of a constitutionally invalid criminal statute with

[*51*]

a resultant chilling effect on first amendment rights. The Court did, however, allow for the possibility that some other, undefined "unusual circumstance" might some day come along that would exert an equally strong pull on the court's sense of equitable justice.

(ii) *Injunction Against Criminal Prosecution— Injury to Property Rights*

The 1908 case of Ex parte Young, 209 U.S. 123 (1908), opened the federal door to enjoining prosecution under an unconstitutional criminal statute where the petitioner suffers irreparable injury to *property* rights. In that case, the petitioner claimed that a state statute fixing railroad rates was confiscatory, and that the legal remedy of the criminal process was inadequate because the extreme severity of penalties provided for violation of the rate statute discouraged any challenge of it by violation. Anyone covered by the unconstitutional statute found that the only "safe course" was to obey it rather than risk an adverse decision on its constitutionality and suffer the enormous penalties. The court found the damage irreparable and enjoined enforcement of the unconstitutional statute.

(iii) *Injunction Against Civil Litigation*

Equity courts are less hesitant to enjoin civil litigation than criminal litigation, partly because the public interest is not as seriously jeopardized. There remains, however, the reluctance of one court to interfere with the proceedings of another. The usual case in which an injunction is granted involves one of two types of situation. In the first, the court of equity enjoins actions against a petitioner in other courts in order to insure that the entire subject of the litigation will be disposed of in the action pending before that court. This includes the typical bill of peace, whereby the court protects the petitioner against multiple actions by a number of respondents in various courts on causes of action arising out of the same transaction. For example, in Yuba Consolidated Gold Fields v. Kilkeary, 206 F.2d 884 (9th Cir.1953), the petitioner was threatened with civil actions by more than 2,000 separate land owners for damages suffered in a flood allegedly caused by the petitioner's negligence in maintaining a wall. The petitioner asked the court to enjoin the prospective plaintiffs from bringing their legal actions in any forum other than that particular federal district court. This type of bill of peace is necessary wherever the same result cannot be achieved by a procedure of consolidation. The relevant harm to the petitioner lies in having to try the same issues of negligence and liability in over 2,000 separate cases, with the resultant disproportionate drain on the petitioner's war chest. The seriousness of the

② Prevents respondent from abusing legal process to gain unfair advantage

harm depends upon the number of potential actions and the availability of consolidation. (In the third phase of the court's decision (discussed in Chapter IV), this harm is balanced against the inconvenience to the respondents of losing the choice of forum and timing, and possible loss of a jury trial. The court will also consider technical difficulty to the court in trying the multiple actions in one suit.)

The second type of case, ripe for an injunction against civil action, is one in which the respondent is deliberately misusing the legal process to harass the petitioner or to gain an unfair advantage. For example, in Usen v. Usen, 136 Me. 480, 13 A.2d 738 (1940), a wife brought a bill in equity in Maine to enjoin her husband from suing for divorce in Florida, where he was fraudulently claiming domicile. The wife could only contest the jurisdiction of the Florida court by making the trip to Florida, and once the divorce decree was entered she could not have it set aside by any of the courts of their true domicile, Maine. She alleged that her husband was fraudulently using the legal process of Florida to place her at an unfair disadvantage, and on this basis, the Maine Court enjoined the husband from proceeding with the Florida action.

A different type of example within this same category occurred in Brewer v. King, 139 Cal. App.2d 33, 293 P.2d 126 (1956), where the wife of the deceased contested his will and brought six separate law suits and four appeals against his heirs on practically the same cause of action. In all of these she was unsuccessful. At this point, the court agreed that she was using the legal process purely for harassment and granted an injunction against her filing any future process on the same cause of action. Cases in which this type of relief is granted are scarce, since the court will require a very clear showing that the respondent is actually *abusing* the right to file legal action before it will block his access to the court system.

An indication of the complex elements that can affect a court's discretion in enjoining prosecution of an action in another court is seen in James v. Grand Trunk Western R. Co., 14 Ill.2d 356, 152 N.E.2d 858 (1959). The petitioner, as administratrix of her deceased husband's estate, brought an action in Illinois against the railroad for the wrongful death of her husband. The respondent railroad obtained an *ex parte* injunction in Michigan against her continuing the action in Illinois. The petitioner then asked the Illinois equity court to enjoin the railroad from enforcing the Michigan injunction. The Illinois court considered the following conflicting criteria in reaching its decision: 1) the petitioner stated and substantiated a claim that she could not get a fair trial in the Michigan court on her legal action;

2) exercise of the power to interfere with individuals proceeding with action within a sister state's jurisdiction was a matter of "great delicacy" and was to be invoked with "great restraint to avoid distressing conflicts and reciprocal interference with jurisdiction;" 3) the recognized principle of comity between states is that the jurisdiction in which a particular action has been filed *first* is to be accorded deference in allowing that jurisdiction to try the action; and 4) although the Michigan injunction was in form directed at the petitioner, its intended effect was to prevent Illinois from trying an action over which it had proper jurisdiction.   The majority declined to heed the warning of Justice Schaefer (dissenting) that when two courts become involved in exchanging barrages by way of injunctions in a conflict over which state is to try the action, the rights of the parties tend to be lost in the scuffle.   The majority ruled that the counter injunction was to be issued.   While the plight of the petitioner undoubtedly set the stage for the decision, the opinion of the majority makes it clear that it was reaction to the Michigan court's insult to its jurisdiction that exerted the prime influence.   Whether, or to what extent, the injunction actually benefited the petitioner is unclear, since she had already been replaced as administratrix of the estate by the Michigan court.

h. EXCEPTION

There is one exception to the conclusion that equity will feel free to move on to other considerations in deciding whether or not to grant an injunction once it has concluded that there is no adequate remedy at law. That is the instance in which, inadequate as the legal remedy may be, equity could do no better. If, for example, the only duty on the part of the respondent is to pay a sum of money under contract, and the legal remedy is inadequate because the respondent is insolvent, equity will not take the field if equitable relief would be equally *ineffective.*

2. EQUITY WILL NOT ENJOIN CRIMINAL CONDUCT

The second principle is generally stated so cryptically that it can be misleading. It is that *equity will not enjoin a crime.* Diamond v. Diamond, 372 Pa. 562, 94 A.2d 569 (1953). A considerable gloss is necessary to bring out the complex meaning of this phrase.

Early in the history of equity jurisdiction, chancellors would regularly grant injunctions to prevent criminal acts of violence as the only protection for the person or property of a private suitor. The equitable remedy ceased, however, when the legal process, notably the Court of Star

Chamber, became active in the enforcement of law and order. From that time on, equity has felt constrained to observe the principle that it would not interfere in the enforcement of the criminal law.

The true thrust of the principle today can best be appreciated by expressing it in this way: equity will not enjoin conduct merely *because* it violates a criminal statute. On the other hand, if the conduct to be enjoined amounts to a nuisance, equity will not be prevented from enjoining it merely because it is criminal activity, as long as it can be shown that the criminal process does not provide an adequate remedy for the petitioner.

When the court is presented with a petition to enjoin activity which violates a criminal statute, it reasons to a decision by the following route.

a.   DOES THE ACTIVITY AMOUNT TO A NUISANCE?

A nuisance can be one of two types for these purposes—public or private. A public nuisance is any activity that is harmful to the health, morals, safety or welfare of the community, or at least such part of the community as must necessarily come into contact with it. People ex rel. Bennett v. Laman, 277 N.Y. 368, 14 N.E.2d 439 (1938); Dean v. State, 151 Ga. 371, 106 S.E. 792 (1921). An action to enjoin a public nuisance must be instituted by a public officer representing the community, such as the attorney general of a state. No private citizen has standing to act as a little attorney general in bringing the action on behalf of the community or state to enjoin a public nuisance.

A private nuisance, is conduct that causes harm to an individual different from that suffered by the general public. In Crawford v. Tyrrell, 128 N.Y. 341, 28 N.E. 514 (1891), for example, the court held that a house of prostitution amounted to a private nuisance to the party living next door. "The indecent conduct of the occupants of the defendant's house, and the noise therefrom, inasmuch as they rendered the plaintiff's house unfit for comfortable or respectable occupation, and unfit for the purposes it was intended for, were facts which constituted a nuisance, and were sufficient grounds for the maintenance of the action." On showing harm different from that suffered by the community, the private individual has standing to seek an injunction.

In deciding whether or not particular conduct amounts to a nuisance, public or private, the fact that it is in violation of a criminal statute is considered neutral and immaterial. People ex rel. Bennett v. Laman, 277 N.Y. 368, 14 N.E.2d 439 (1938). In State v. Red Owl Stores, Inc., 262 Minn. 31, 115 N.W.2d 643 (1962), for example, a state statute made it a crime for anyone other than a registered pharmacist to sell such products as Bufferin and Alka-Seltzer. The attorney general sought to enjoin a chain of retail food stores from selling these products, claiming that the criminal statute established *prima facie* proof that the public suffered a harm from that activity. The court held, on retrial, that the criminal statute could provide no such presumption, and that the state had, in fact, failed to prove any substantial danger to the public.

One limited exception to the rule of immateriality of the criminal statute is found in State ex rel. Abbott v. House of Vision-Belgard-Spero, 259 Wis. 87, 47 N.W.2d 321 (1951). The defendant company hired unlicensed people to practice optometry on its behalf and widely advertised their services as superior to those of licensed optometrists in the community. The court held in that case that a nuisance exists if a criminal statute is being "openly, publicly, persistently and intentionally" violated.

b. IS THE LEGAL REMEDY BY WAY OF ENFORCEMENT OF THE CRIMINAL STATUTE ADEQUATE?

Courts have found the legal remedy inadequate to alleviate a public or private nuisance in a number of different situations. In State v. Preuss, 217 Minn. 100, 13 N.W.2d 774 (1944), the court found that the criminal penalties imposed on the respondent in the course of 25 convictions of violating the statute prohibiting the sale of liquor were ineffective in compelling him to abate the nuisance. In City of Tupelo v. Walton, 237 Miss. 892, 116 So.2d 808 (1960), the criminal fines imposed in 66 convictions for violating the law against opening a store on Sunday did not compare with the profit to be made, and could therefore be absorbed as cost of doing business.

In State v. Red Owl Stores, Inc., 253 Minn. 236, 92 N.W.2d 103 (1958), the court found that the alleged nuisance consisted of innumerable misdemeanors in the sale of drugs like Alka-Seltzer through hundreds of retail stores across a large portion of the state. The confirmed policy of the respondent was to insist on a jury trial and proof beyond a reasonable doubt as to each particular violation for the purpose of preventing effective enforcement of the statute. In an action for equitable relief against the alleged nuisance caused by these sales, the court found the legal remedy inadequate.

In Commonwealth ex rel. Attorney General v. Pollitt, 258 Ky. 489, 80 S.W.2d 543 (1935), the respondent was practicing dentistry without a license, but his popularity in the community was apparently such that in spite of direct testimony as to his operation, the grand jury would not indict him. Therefore the legal remedy by criminal prosecution was ineffective, and inadequate. By comparison, other courts have held that failure of juries to indict or convict is not a circumstance that equity will consider in deciding on the adequacy of the legal remedy. "It is no part of the office of equity to take over the duties of other public officers." People ex rel. Bennett v. Laman, supra. The court here draws the distinction between an attack on the adequacy of a system based on its inability to abate the nuisance, even when operating at peak efficiency, and an attack based on its internal flaws and inefficiencies.

One current reason, in addition to the adequacy of the legal remedy, for the court's reluctance to enjoin criminal activity, is the danger of shortcutting the constitutional protections an individual would have as a defendant in a criminal action instead of as a respondent in an equity action. If the defendant is tried criminally, he has the right to an attorney, court-appointed if necessary, the right to insist on proof beyond a reasonable doubt, and all of the constitutional rights of defendants that have been applied in both state and federal courts. If, through the injunctive process, a defendant can be subjected to contempt sanctions for the same conduct without the inconvenience of affording him those rights, there is danger that the injunctive process could be abused for that purpose. In this case, courts feel that expediency and efficiency in abating a nuisance might be won at too high a price to individual rights.

This fear has been considerably alleviated since the Supreme Court decided, in In re Oliver, 333 U.S. 257 (1948), that a defendant in any criminal contempt proceeding has the right to have a public hearing, to have reasonable notice of the charge against him, to examine witnesses against him, to testify in his own behalf, and to be represented by counsel. In Bloom v. Illinois, 391 U.S. 194 (1968), the Supreme Court held that in any non-petty criminal contempt hearing, the defendant has the right to a trial by jury, even though the contempt may have been committed in the presence of the trial judge. The Court stated broadly that, "We cannot say that the need to further respect for judges and courts is entitled to more consideration than the interest of the individual not to be subjected to serious criminal punishment without the benefit of all the procedural protections worked out carefully over the years and deemed fundamental to our system of justice."

This would indicate that in time, a criminal contempt hearing will resemble a criminal trial in every particular. This will, however, still leave two important differences between the injunctive and criminal processes. First, the typical criminal statute fixes the maximum penalty that can be imposed for its violation. There is generally no limit, other than the standard of abuse of discretion, on the penalty that can be imposed in criminal contempt. Secondly, the respondent under an injunction can usually be reached through civil, as well as criminal contempt sanctions, and the constitutional safeguards discussed here do not apply in civil contempt. (See discussion of Civil Contempt below).

3. EQUITY PROTECTS ONLY PROPERTY RIGHTS

No derivative rights

Most legal historians accept the theory that an unfortunate dictum of Lord Eldon in Gee v. Pritchard, 2 Swanston 402, Ch. 1818, was the source of the principle that equity will protect only property rights and will not lend its sanctions to the protection of personal rights. In that case, the plaintiff sought to prevent the publication of private letters written by her deceased husband, a former clergyman. Counsel for the petitioner argued that the grounds for seeking the injunction were that publication of the letters would be "painful to the feelings of the plaintiff." Lord Eldon interposed:

> "I will relieve you also from that argument. The question will be, whether the bill has stated facts of which the Court can take notice, as a case of civil property, which it is bound to protect. The injunction cannot be maintained on any principle of this sort, that if a letter has been written in the way of

> friendship, either the continuance or the discontinuance of that friendship affords a reason for the interference of the Court."

Subsequent courts and judges took up this obscure, somewhat ambiguous comment and turned it into an iron-clad rule that has hobbled the development of equitable relief for injury to personal rights from that time on. The great misfortune, as many courts recognize today, is that there has never been any sound reason or justification for the principle. It was simply accepted without question as if handed down from above. Noted commentators, such as Spence in his work on Equitable Jurisdiction (1849), and Kerr in his work on Injunctions (1871), aided in its perpetuation by recognizing it as an accepted principle.

Through the years of its existence, however, while courts were faithfully canting the principle, it is possible that it may have been made to seem more restricting than it actually was. No case has been found in which equitable relief was denied *solely* on the ground that a personal right, rather than property right, was concerned. In each case denying relief, a substantial alternative ground was present, such as existence of an adequate remedy at law. In other cases, the additional reason consisted of a failure to prove great or irreparable harm. (See e.g., Douglas v. City of Jeannette, 319 U.S. 157 (1943), or an inability of the court to devise any remedy that would not be impractical to administer. (See e. g., Snedaker v. King, 111 Ohio St. 225, 145 N.E. 15 (1924)).

The current state of the principle, as many cases have noted, is that it is observed more in the breach than in the observance. Courts have taken two different approaches in laying it to rest. The more honest of the two is the direct approach taken by the Massachusetts court in Kenyon v. City of Chicopee, 320 Mass. 528, 70 N.E.2d 241 (1946). In that case, ten Jehovah's Witnesses sought to enjoin the city and several of its officials from interfering with their freedom of religion, speech, and press, by prosecuting them under a local littering ordinance for distributing leaflets. The defendants demurred solely on the ground that no property rights of the petitioners were jeopardized. The court was rightly impressed by the argument of petitioners that if equity would safeguard their right to sell bananas, it should be at least equally solicitous of their Constitutional rights of freedom of speech, press and religion. The court held squarely that, "Equity will protect personal rights by injunction upon the same conditions upon which it will protect property rights . . . ."

The courts of a number of other jurisdictions, such as New Jersey, Delaware, New York, Ohio and California have followed the straightforward approach of the *Kenyon* decision. Other courts have done so with the enabling hand of legislation, such as Article 2989 of the Revised Statutes of Texas, which provides that equity judges may grant injunctions in *any* case "Where it shall appear that the party applying for said writ is entitled to the relief demanded, and such relief or any part thereof requires the restraining of some act prejudicial to the applicant." Ex parte Warfield, 40 Tex.Crim. 413, 50 S.W. 933 (1899). In Oklahoma, a similar statute has been interpreted "to provide for injunctive relief against injuries to a plaintiff as well as injuries to a plaintiff's property." Nation v. Chism, 154 Okl. 50, 6 P.2d 766 (1932).

It is interesting that the English system of law that forged and then exported to America this blind restriction managed to cut its own Gordian knot decisively as early as 1873 by legislation which gave power to the English court of equity to grant injunctions in *all* cases in which it should appear to the court to be just that such order should be made. Act of 1873, § 25, subdiv. 8.

The second approach arrives at the same result by a less courageous, less reasoned course, and has been by far the more common path chosen by courts seeking to obviate the principle in deserving cases. That approach is to recognize the principle, pay it lip service, and then go on to discover, create, or fictionalize some "property interest", no matter how far-fetched, on which to justify the granting of an injunction to protect personal rights. In the original case of Gee v. Pritchard itself, Lord Eldon laid down the rule, and then proceeded to duck under it by finding a "property" right of the petitioner in the letters, which he then felt justified in protecting by injunction.

This fictional approach has been followed by numerous courts in protection of an infinite variety of personal interests under the guise of "property rights." These personal interests have included, for example, reputation, privacy, health, physical comfort, marital security, and education, custody and names of children.

The major drawback of this indirect approach, as compared with the straightforward reversal of the principle, has been the uncertainty in predicting whether or not a court would be sufficiently moved by a particular case to "discover" a property interest, and thereby open another area of personal rights to the protection of the equity court. Under the direct approach, no such uncertainty exists. Once the petitioner demonstrates a threat to any recognized right, personal or property, he can be granted whatever injunctive protection the court finds appropriate.

As courts of equity have become more inclined to openly protect personal interests, they have shown an increasing willingness to recognize dif-

[*68*]

ferent types of injuries to personal interests. These tend to divide into three categories: 1) violation of civil rights; 2) violation of legally recognized "rights of privacy"; and 3) certain injuries to purely personal feelings or sensitivities.

a. VIOLATION OF CIVIL RIGHTS

With the increase in sensitivity to constitutionally guaranteed civil rights, courts of equity soon realized that, for example, the damage to a child's education caused by a local school system shackled by segregation was as clear a case of irreparable injury as any loss of property. It became equally clear that the only conceivable remedy lay in injunctive relief. Out of this realization came the string of decisions from Brown v. Board of Education, 349 U.S. 294 (1955), to Swann v. Charlotte-Mecklenburg Board of Education, 402 U.S. 1 (1971), through which the courts prescribed and guided a program for eradicating school segregation. At each stage, individual rights to a non-segregated school system had to be balanced against a realistic concern for the affect of predictable disruption on the public welfare, and this imposed a restraint on the speed with which the court could demand full compliance with its ultimate order. It was in the nature of the problem that interim orders of the court were required with each new development, in order to give practical effect to the court's initial command of compliance "with all deliberate speed." The fact that the court was willing to undertake the difficult and lengthy process of step by step supervision of this politically explosive program indicates the degree of importance that had come to be attached to violation of constitutionally guaranteed civil rights.

In other areas of civil rights, courts began applying injunctive relief against what came to be considered irreparable injury in loss of voting rights, Hamer v. Campbell, 358 F.2d 215 (5th Cir.1966), segregation of public accommodations, Everett v. Harron, 380 Pa. 123, 110 A.2d 383 (1955), and interference with freedom of speech, Burnside v. Byars, 363 F.2d 744 (5th Cir.1966). The shift from protection solely of property rights to the undisguised protection of personal interests received its strongest impetus in the area of constitutional rights.

b. VIOLATION OF RIGHTS OF PRIVACY

As courts of law began to fashion common law actions for damages in new areas generally termed "rights of privacy," equity courts followed closely in providing injunctive protection for these newly recognized rights. It was not difficult, for example, to discover irreparable injury in the unauthorized use of a petitioner's name or picture for its commercial value in advertising a product, since a) the amount of monetary damage was unmeasurable, and b) once the privacy of the individual was invaded it could never again be restored. One iron-clad exception is that the court will not enjoin an injury to the right of privacy based merely upon a libelous or slanderous defamation because of the greater concern for the respondent's right to freedom of speech. In such cases, regardless of the irreparability of the petitioner's injury, he is relegated to a legal action for damages.

c. INJURY TO PERSONAL FEELINGS

Equity courts have historically refused to afford relief where the only injury claimed was to the petitioner's personal feelings or sensibilities. For example, in Baumann v. Baumann, 250 N.Y. 382, 165 N.E. 819 (1929), the respondent secured a Mexican divorce from the petitioner and married the second respondent. The petitioner sought a declaratory judgment to the effect that the divorce and subsequent marriage were void, and an injunction against the respondents' representing themselves to be husband and wife. The only injury caused to the petitioner by the conduct of the respondents was annoyance and humiliation. The court granted the declaratory judgment but denied the injunction. Although the acts of the respondents were illegal, as well as "socially and morally wrong," the court would not restrain "conduct which merely injures a person's feelings and causes mental anguish." Similarly, in Hodecker v. Stricker, 39 N.Y.S. 515 (1896), the court refused to enjoin the respondent from living with the petitioner's husband and calling herself "Mrs. Hodecker" on the ground that "obligations, rights, and duties merely moral are not the subject of equitable relief."

The reasons for this limitation have been twofold. First, it is generally true that where the conduct to be enjoined injures personal feelings only, any decree that would afford adequate protection would, as a practical matter, be extremely difficult to enforce. Secondly, as stated by the court in *Baumann,* "Attempts to govern the morals of people by injunctions can only result in making ridiculous the courts which grant such decrees." The courts are not anxious to assume the role of arbiters on delicate points of public morality.

There were, however, isolated instances in which the appeal of the petitioner's case induced the court to overlook this limitation. For example, in 1875, the Arkansas court enjoined the disturbance of a burial lot. While the court could have hidden its rationale in a discussion of real property interests, it chose to ground its decision squarely on personal interests:

> "The extent of the injury to be inflicted must depend upon the sympathies and feel-

ings of the parties injured, and their peculiar views as to the sacredness of the spot where the remains rest. Whilst it might be a matter of little moment to some, it might inflict an irreparable injury to others, which money could not compensate." Mooney v. Cooledge, 30 Ark. 640 (1875).

While cases of this kind were extremely rare in the past, as equity courts withdraw further from the personal rights v. property rights distinction, they are showing less hesitancy to grant relief where personal feelings are concerned. There is as yet no discernible pattern to the conglomeration of areas in which courts have broken down the barriers. One primary area for this kind of court activity is that of family relations. For example, it is not uncommon for courts to enter the type of injunction granted in Mark v. Kahn, 333 Mass. 517, 131 N.E.2d 758 (1956), whereby the former wife of the petitioner was enjoined from changing the name of their child.

Other areas in which courts have protected personal feelings defy categorization, and seem to stand as a growing body of isolated exceptions to the old limitation. The one common element seems to be that in each case the court was sufficiently moved by the petitioner's situation to overcome the now weakened restraint of that limitation.

4. EQUITY WILL NOT ENJOIN A LIBEL

The principle that *equity will not enjoin a libel* is similar to the principle that equity will not enjoin a crime. The court will not be persuaded to grant an injunction simply because the threatened communication is libelous, for reasons to be explored below; but if sufficient independent grounds exist for granting the injunction, the court will not be stymied by the fact that the conduct amounts to a libel. The origin of the principle goes back to a time when jurisdiction over cases of libel was left to the Court of Star Chamber in England, which exercised that jurisdiction by employing the sanctions of cutting off ears, slitting noses, and branding foreheads, in addition to the granting of injunctions.

Even after the abolition of the Star Chamber, courts of equity have continued to adhere to the principle that equity would not enjoin a libel. Five distinct reasons have been given for its perpetuation.

a. CONSTITUTIONAL RIGHTS TO FREEDOM OF SPEECH AND PRESS

According to Blackstone, whose views on the common law were generally accepted in this country at the time of the formation of the Bill

[74]

of Rights, freedom of speech and of the press meant freedom from any sort of *prior restraint* on the dissemination of speech or writings, as distinguished from civil or criminal liability following libelous, or other improper communications. The impact of the Constitutional provisions therefore, falls squarely on the preventive remedy of injunction. There are, however, types of speech that are not protected by the Constitution. For example, speech used to coerce or unlawfully intimidate, and speech used with the purpose or effect of interfering with the course of justice fall outside of that protection. It is these exceptions that allow the court to enjoin certain communications in the particular circumstances to be discussed below.

b. EQUITY PROTECTS PROPERTY RIGHTS AND NOT PERSONAL RIGHTS

This principle, discussed at length above, is responsible, in those jurisdictions that continue to adhere to it, for the denial of injunctions against libelous speech that takes its toll on personal rights and sensibilities as opposed to property interests. Even among those dwindling jurisdictions, however, courts of equity have strained to find some property concept in a deserving case on which to justify the granting of an injunction. For example, in Gee v. Pritchard, supra, Lord Eldon granted an injunction against the publication of certain personal letters that would cause embarrassment to the petitioner by rationalizing a "property" value in the letters appropriate for protection by the court. The court seemed to feel that this obscure, fictionalized property right justified issuance of an injunction which it felt it could not properly issue for the protection of the real interest of the petitioner,—the honor of the deceased and the sensibilities of his family and friends.

c. RIGHT TO JURY TRIAL

Courts have also cited the right of the defendant to a jury decision on the truth of the alleged libel as an additional ground for denying the injunction. This concern has diminished with the procedural advances made in recent years in combining courts of law and equity so that the granting of a jury trial on specific issues raised in an otherwise equitable proceeding is a matter of relatively small inconvenience.

d. CRIMINAL CONDUCT

The problems raised in the discussion of the principle that Equity will not enjoin a crime overlap here, since in many jurisdictions certain types of libel violate criminal statutes. The considerations that allow the court to ignore the criminality of the act and issue an injunction in spite of that principle (as discussed above) apply equally here.

e. ADEQUACY OF REMEDY AT LAW

Since in a true libel situation, an action at law for money damages will lie, the petitioner must sustain the burden of proving that the legal remedy is inadequate. See Murphy v. Daytona Beach Humane Society, 176 So.2d 922 (Fla.App.1965). In this area, however, it is generally not difficult to establish that inadequacy, since it is the highly unusual case in which the amount of damages from a libel can be calculated. Even cases involving disparagement of a business or trade product do not lend themselves to any reasonable calculation of damages, and therefore the legal remedy is seldom adequate.

These five considerations continue to support the court's refusal to enjoin a communication simply because of its libelous nature. Courts are, however, willing to grant injunctive relief where there is the additional tortious element of *conspiracy, intimidation* or *coercion*, the publication of the words being merely an instrument and incident. Warren House Co. v. Handwerger, 240 Md. 177, 213 A.2d 574 (1965). For example, in Gompers v. Bucks Stove & Range Co,, 221 U.S. 418 (1911), the court stated that while it would not enjoin libelous conduct *per se*, it would enjoin an unlawful boycott accomplished through libelous publications. The conspiratorial nature of the activity, causing irreparable injury to the business of the petitioner, was the key to side-stepping the rule against enjoining a libel.

In American Mercury v. Chase, 13 F.2d 224 (D.Mass.1926), a publisher sought an injunction against the Watch and Ward Society's threats to distributors that if they handled books of the publisher which the Society considered unlawful, criminal prosecution would follow. The effect of such threats on the sale of the book had been shown to be serious. The court issued an injunction against these libelous threats because of the additional elements of intimidation and coercion. Similarly, in Dehydro, Inc. v. Tretolite Co., 53 F. 2d 273 (N.D.Okla.1931) the court enjoined a competitor of the petitioner from making written and oral statements to petitioner's customers to the effect that petitioner's product infringed the competitor's patent, and that the customers would render themselves liable in damages if they used the product. The basis for the injunction was not the libel, but the coercion and intimidation amounting to unfair competition accomplished by means of the libel. By comparison, in American Malting Co. v. Keitel, 217 F. 672 (D.C.N.Y.1914), the court denied an injunction against defamation which was intended only to produce feelings of anger and hatred for the petitioner and his product. The court drew a distinction between the "mere defamer, and one who has or pretends to have power to injure the persons to whom he publishes his defamations."

New York courts have liberalized the granting of injunctions to include any case in which the respondent acts willfully with the intent of injuring plaintiff's business. In Old Investors' and Traders' Corp. v. Jenkins, 133 Misc. 213, 232 N. Y.S. 245 (1928), for example, the court enjoined false publications regarding petitioner's business by a competitor, although there was no element of coercion, intimidation or conspiracy. The deliberate intent to engage in unfair competition was enough to remove the case from one of "mere publication of a libel" which the court would not enjoin. In Advance Music Corp. v. American Tobacco Co., 296 N.Y. 79, 70 N.E.2d 401 (1946), the court went one step further by holding that the petitioner had stated a cause of action in alleging that the radio show, "Your Hit Parade", had deliberately placed petitioner's songs lower on the list of the weeks' 10 most popular songs than they deserved, with the intent of injuring plaintiff's business. Here there was no allegation of conspiracy, intimidation or coercion, or even unfair competition—merely the alleged deliberate intent to injure petitioner's business.

What minor liberalization has occurred through the courts in the granting of injunctions against deliberate injury by false publications seems confined to the area of "trade libels",—disparagement of a product or business, usually for the motive of unfair competition. There has been practically no relaxing of the principle against enjoining libelous injury to personal interests.

Another source of liberalization of the common law limitations has been statutes empowering the court to enjoin certain communications. For example, in Brown v. State Realty Co., 304 F.Supp. 1236 (N.D.Ga.1969), the court granted an injunction against the respondent's making further statements in violation of 42 U.S.C. § 3604(e) which made it unlawful "For profit, to induce or attempt to induce any person to sell or rent any dwelling by representations regarding the entry or prospective entry into the neighborhood of a person or persons of a particular race, color, religion, or national origin." The defendants had been engaging in "block busting", i. e., inducing quick sales of homes at reduced prices by making statements regarding the entry of minority families into neighborhood. The effect of the statute is to remove from the court's consideration the five objections to injunctive relief listed above, and to leave the court free to grant an injunction where it is found necessary in order to compel compliance with the statute.

Similarly, under Section 5 of the Federal Trade Commission Act, 15 U.S.C.A. § 45, the federal courts of appeals are empowered to grant injunctions for the purpose of enforcing orders of the Federal Trade Commission against "Unfair methods of competition".

5. EQUITY WILL NOT ISSUE A DECREE IT CANNOT ENFORCE

One general principle has grown out of the concern of courts of equity for the preservation of their image and prestige. To avoid embarrassment to its own dignity, a court of equity will generally exercise its discretion to deny a decree that would be impractical for the court to enforce. These situations fall mainly into three categories: a) inability to bring enforcement pressures to bear on the respondent because he is likely to absent himself and his property from the jurisdiction; b) difficulty of enforcing an order that must be carried out in another jurisdiction; and c) inability of the court to supervise an order that requires special skill or ability, or that requires performance over an extended period of time.

① Our of jurisdiction — pressure on resp. dig.
② Another jurisdiction
③ Prolonged supervision

a. RESPONDENT IS LIKELY TO PLACE HIMSELF AND HIS PROPERTY BEYOND THE POWER OF THE COURT

In this situation it is assumed that the court has acquired personal jurisdiction over the respondent. It can, however, be a fleeting, illusory power if, as a practical matter, the respondent is likely to flee the jurisdiction and leave the court powerless to enforce its injunction by means of contempt sanctions. Such situations would breed disrespect for the court's orders, and therefore the court will exercise its discretion in refusing to grant the injunction.

In deciding whether or not the respondent is likely to place the court in this position of impotence, the court will consider the respondent's roots in the jurisdiction, such as a home, family, stable employment, and any ties that would make flight for this purpose impractical. The court will also consider the existence of property of the respondent with some permanence in the jurisdiction, such as real estate, on which a contempt fine might be executed. The court will then take into account any indication of the intent of the respondent to exercise his mobility to escape the reach of the court's power, because it is only in cases in which there is some indication of respondent's intent to flee that the court's concern is aroused over the potential loss of respect from

[*82*]

a respondent's ability to disobey its order with impugnity.

In DeBeers Consolidated Mines, Ltd. v. United States, 325 U.S. 212 (1945), the petitioner requested an order of the court sequestering respondent's property at the institution of the bill for equitable relief in order to insure that the court would have leverage over the respondent in case the court should issue the injunction sought and the respondent should flee the jurisdiction to escape enforcement. The property sought to be sequestered had no direct relation to the injunction asked in the bill, but was merely to be used as a means of keeping the respondent subject to the court's order. The Supreme Court held that such sequestration of a respondent's property would be improper because the purpose to be served was too remote from the means employed, and the allowance of this interim remedy would impose on the respondent too severe a hardship over the indefinite period of the life of the requested injunction. This case has been consistently followed.

One rather limited method of preventing the respondent from escaping enforcement of the court's order is use of the writ of *ne exeat* ("that he might not depart"). This is an ancient extraordinary writ, whereby the respondent is taken into custody until he gives a bond, or bail, fixed by the court, conditioned on his remaining subject to the enforcement processes of the court. Its use is extremely limited in two ways: 1) it is only allowed in cases in which a fixed debt or duty to account is owed by the respondent to the petitioner, or the suit is to preserve certain property; and 2) because of the extreme nature of the writ, it is issued only upon proof of the respondent's intention to flee the court's enforcement of its injunction.

The reason that courts are so aware of the territorial limits of their effective power is that the doctrine of full faith and credit under the Constitution does not apply to discretionary decrees, such as injunctions. A petitioner cannot simply take his decree and follow the respondent into another jurisdiction and there have it enforced. See Union Pacific R. Co. v. Rule, 155 Minn. 302, 193 N.W. 161 (1923). (The subject of extraterritorial effect of an equity decree will be discussed below).

b. EXECUTION OF THE DECREE WILL REQUIRE THE RESPONDENT TO ACT OUTSIDE OF THE COURT'S JURISDICTION

In this situation the court is concerned with several problems. The first is the practical difficulty of the court's supervising or monitoring the execution of its decree in another territorial jurisdiction. The second is the embarrassment that would result from an inability to enforce its or-

1) Difficulty 'fc pupun   [84]

2) Embarrassed if ymcid

3) Conflicting laws in other   jurisdiction

ders. The third is the possibility of collision of the court's order with conflicting policies or laws (particularly zoning and building codes in relevant situations) of the jurisdiction in which execution is to take place.

Generally the court will not hesitate in granting a decree calling for action outside the state where that action will affect property of the petitioner within the state, as long as the court has reason to believe that the respondent will remain subject to the court's power. See Salton Sea Cases, 172 F. 792 (9th Cir. 1909). Where, however, out of state action is to be required to benefit property of the petitioner which is also out of state, the court will generally apply this principle and deny relief, relegating the petitioner to the jurisdiction in which the property is located. An exception occurred in Alexander v. Tolleston Club, 110 Ill. 65 (1884), where the court enjoined the respondent from trespassing on the out of state property of the petitioner. The court noted that both parties would remain subject to the court's power, and no *affirmative* act of the respondent which the court might find it difficult to supervise would be required.

The court in Madden v. Rosseter, 114 Misc. 416, 187 N.Y.S. 462 (1921) was induced by the circumstances of the case to carve an even larger exception to this principle. The petitioner and respondent each owned a half interest in a race

[*85*]

horse. The respondent was to have use of the horse for two seasons in California, and the petitioner was then to have use of the horse for two seasons in Kentucky. When his time was up, the respondent refused to surrender possession of the horse as agreed. Since time was of the essence, and the equities lay clearly on the side of the petitioner, the court ordered the respondent to take the affirmative action, necessarily out of state, of delivering up possession of the horse. The court went further and appointed a receiver to travel to California "and to take appropriate steps there or elsewhere including the invoking of the aid of the courts of that or any other state, or of the Federal courts, to gain possession of the animal and ship him to the plaintiff's stock farm in Kentucky." The court realized that the power of its appointed officer ceased at the state line. The court felt however, that the petitioners cause deserved relief, and *no state or Federal court could give more complete relief than the court of New York*. The court concluded its opinion with the hope that "The courts of sister states may be relied upon to aid in serving the ends of justice whenever our own process falls short of effectiveness."

c. IF THE INJUNCTION WERE GRANTED THE COURT WOULD BE REQUIRED TO SUPERVISE PERFORMANCE EXTENDING OVER A LENGTHY PERIOD OF TIME OR INVOLVING SPECIAL SKILLS OR KNOWLEDGE

Under this category there are three distinct types of situations which have in common the feature of serious *difficulty of supervision* of the respondent's performance by the court which could render the order futile and an embarrassment to the dignity of the court.

(i) *Performance over a Long Period of Time*

The first type of case in which the court will refuse to grant an injunction is that in which performance of the order would extend over a long period of time. For example, in King Features Syndicate v. Courrier, 241 Iowa 870, 43 N.W.2d 718 (1950), the court refused to order specific performance of a contract to furnish wire news reports to the petitioner for broadcasting. The court would have been required to oversee continuous performance over an indefinite period of time.

(ii) *Performance of Special Skills*

The second type involves cases wherein the court is asked to order the respondent to perform

[87]

personal services calling for special skills or training beyond the court's capacity to evaluate. For example, petitions for specific performance of contracts to perform in any of the arts from singing to sculpture are generally denied. The major impediment is the court's confessed inability to judge whether a particular opera singer or painter has given a performance of the quality called for in his contract. DeRivafinoldi v. Corsetti, 4 Paige 264 (N.Y.Ch.1833). This problem is not limited to the arts however. In Rutland Marble Co. v. Ripley, 77 U.S. 339 (1870), the petitioner asked the court to order specific performance of a contract to deliver marble of a certain type, quality, and size. The court refused, partly because it would be called upon to supervise performance over an indefinite period of time, and also because the court did not feel capable of judging the quality of marble.

A second difficulty, present even in cases in which the particular subject matter is within the capacity of the court to evaluate is the danger of subjecting the respondent to involuntary servitude in violation of the 13th Amendment to the Constitution. This turns, to some extent, on how closely the respondent's actions in performance are to be controlled by the petitioner.

[*88*]

Cover, sue for damages.

(iii) *Performance of Building or Repair*

The third type of case has much in common with the second, but because of certain peculiar features, it deserves separate treatment. This category involves petitions for affirmative injunctions to build or repair. Here too the problem is the inability of the court to adequately supervise the performance. Courts of equity have uniformly recognized their inability a) to inform the respondent in adequate detail exactly what kind of building will suffice, b) to judge whether or not the respondent has rendered substantial performance, and c) to determine the measure of damages for any inadequacies of performance. For these reasons, courts have deemed orders to build or repair impracticable. See, e. g., Beck v. Allison, 56 N.Y. 366 (1874). A second ground, commonly joined with this, is the relative adequacy of the remedy at law where the petitioner can simply have the construction performed by another builder and sue the respondent for money damages.

This rule, however, like all others in equity, is not without exceptions. Where the construction called for is of a relatively simple type, understandable to the layman, the principle will not apply. For example, in Jones v. Parker, 163 Mass. 564, 40 N.E. 1044 (1895), the petitioner sought specific performance of a contract to supply heat and light to a building. The court felt capable of

[*89*]

resolving the rather narrow range of difference between the petitioner and respondent as to what would comprise reasonable heating and lighting. This subject did not call for special skill or training, and therefore the court granted relief.

Courts of equity have also carved four specific, narrowly-defined exceptions to the principle in cases of building or repair. The court will generally grant a petition for specific performance of a construction contract where 1) the building is to be done on the land of the person who agreed to do it; 2) the consideration given by the petitioner for the promise to build or repair was conveyance of the land on which the construction was to be done; 3) the petitioner has already executed his obligations under the contract; and 4) the building promised is in some way essential to the use, or contributory to the value of the petitioner's adjoining land. See Zygmunt v. Avenue Realty Co., 108 N.J.Eq. 462, 155 A. 544 (1931).

To each of the three categories of this principle there is one general exception that will override the considerations against granting relief. This exception arises in cases in which a substantial public interest is at stake. "When the inconvenience of the courts in acting is more than counterbalanced by the inconvenience of the public if they do not act, the interest of the public will prevail." Standard Fashion Co. v. Siegel Cooper Co., 157 N.Y. 60, 51 N.E. 408 (1898). For example, in Edison Illuminating Co. v. Eastern Penn. Power Co., 253 Pa. 457, 98 A. 652 (1916), a public utility corporation leased facilities for generating power. Under one term of the leasing contract, the respondent was to keep the facilities in good repair. The petitioner sought specific performance of this term and the court granted relief, stating that:

> "As a general rule, courts will hesitate to order specific performance of contracts where the execution of the decree requires supervision extending over a long period of time, or calls for a knowledge of technical matters, incident to its performance, which neither the court nor its officers may be expected to possess . . . ; but there are a number of cases holding, in effect, that where the contract is one in which public interest and convenience are at stake, specific performance will be decreed even though certain oversight or discretion is required."

This exception applies primarily in cases involving public utilities and agencies of transportation (particularly railroads) which are deemed to promote the general welfare. See, e. g., Joy v. City of St. Louis, 138 U.S. 1 (1890). It can also apply, however, to any case in which a substantial benefit or harm to the public is involved. In Scudder v. Zeckendorf Hotels Corp., 224 N.Y.S.2d 432 (Sup.1961), the court ordered the respondent

hotel to stage a fund-raising dinner in performance of its contract. Without this dinner, a public service organization would have lost its only
annual fund-raising affair. This harm to the
public interest outweighed the difficulty of the
court's supervising such a complex matter as the
production of a banquet.

In some instances the court's willingness to
take on more difficult or lengthy burdens of supervision is effected by the hardship to be caused
to the petitioner if the court does not grant relief.
For example in Texas Co. v. Central Fuel Oil Co.,
194 F. 1 (8th Cir. 1912), the court granted specific performance of a long term agreement by the
respondent to transmit his oil through the petitioner's pipeline. A serious consideration in the
court's decision to grant relief was the fact that
the petitioner had already gone to the trouble of
extending his pipeline to the defendant's wells.
The trend seems to be for courts to continue to
assume more difficult problems of supervision
with the help of competent court-appointed mas-
ters and receivers, as the justice of the case demands. Kearns-Gorsuch Bottle Co. v. Hartford-
Fairmont Co., 1 F.2d 318 (S.D.N.Y.1921).

An indirect method of doing justice to the petitioner while preserving the principal intact in
construction cases was used by Lord Eldon in
Lane v. Newdigate, 10 Vesey 192, Ch. 1804. In
that case, the petitioner leased certain premises

from the respondent for the purpose of erecting mills to be run by a supply of water which the respondent agreed to keep flowing, consistent with his own uses. The petitioner sought to have the court order the respondent to make necessary repairs to his locks and stop-gates to restore the water supply. The court was hesitant to issue an *affirmative* order that the repair work be done because of the principle in building or repair cases; but Lord Eldon obviated the principle by devising a double negative decree. In essence, he ordered the respondent not to continue to *refuse* to abide by his covenant in regard to the supply of water. He stated:

> "The question is, whether the Court can specifically order that to be restored. I think I can direct it in terms, that will have that effect. The Injunction, I shall order, will create the necessity of restoring the Stop-gate; and attention will be had to the manner in which he is to use these locks; and he will find it difficult, I apprehend, to avoid completely repairing these works."

A variation of that device was used in Lumley v. Wagner, 1 DeGex MacNaghten, Gordon 604, Ch.1852. In that case an opera singer contracted to sing at the petitioner's theater and agreed not to use her talents at any other theater during the period of her commitment. She later agreed to sing at a competing theater in violation of her agreement. The petitioner sought specific performance. In accordance with the principle, the court felt that it could not affirmatively order the respondent to perform at the petitioner's theater. It could, however, and did issue a negative decree enjoining the respondent from singing at a competing theater. This device has proven popular with courts in this country wishing to preserve the principle but at the same time to grant some effective relief in particularly deserving cases. Two limitations imposed upon the use of the negative decree are these: 1) The court must find that the parties to the contract agreed that the respondent should be under obligation to refrain from performing services for any other; and 2) The court will only enjoin a respondent from engaging in activity which would be in actual competition with the petitioner's business. For example, in DePol v. Sohlke, 30 N.Y.Super.Ct. 280 (1867), the petitioner sought an injunction against a dancer's violation of an agreement to perform at petitioner's theater by performing instead in a theater in another city. The court denied the negative injunction because it found that the two theaters involved were not in actual competition with each other; and the court would not issue the negative order simply to compel the respondent indirectly to perform his affirmative agreement.

6. EQUITY WILL NOT ISSUE AN INJUNCTION WHICH CANNOT BE REDUCED TO TERMS SPECIFIC ENOUGH TO INFORM THE RESPONDENT OF WHAT IS REQUIRED

Because an injunction carries with it the threat of the criminal contempt sanctions of fine or imprisonment for its violation, equity courts have adopted a principle analogous to the rule that one cannot be convicted of a crime unless the statute defines clearly and definitely what the defendant can and cannot do. In certain cases, because of the nature of the fact situation, it is impossible for the court to frame an injunction that will accomplish the purpose of the order and at the same time adequately inform the respondent of the specific acts that are commanded or forbidden. For example, in Lynch v. Uhlenhopp, 248 Iowa 68, 78 N.W.2d 491 (1956), two parties obtaining a divorce entered into a stipulation which was incorporated into the decree. One of the terms was that the five year old son of the parties, who was to remain in the custody of the mother, a non-Catholic, was to be "reared in the Roman Catholic Religion". The husband later filed a petition to hold the wife in contempt for violating that term. The court reversed the original order on the grounds that "[a] judgment must be definite and certain in itself, or capable of being made so by proper construction. It must fix clearly the rights and liabilities of the respective parties to the cause, *and be such as defendant may readily understand* and be capable of performing . . .." The problem was deeper than merely re-phrasing the decree with more specificity. It is a practical impossibility to devise a written order that would adequately direct a non-Catholic on all of the intangible details involved in a good faith effort to raise a child in the Catholic religion (including conversation at home, cooperation with church or parochial school personnel, and all that goes beyond the pure formalistic attendance at services). No adequate order could be drawn, and therefore none should be issued.

In this area, discretion meets and overlaps constitutional limitation. If the order is so vague or uncertain that it would be a denial of due process to enforce it through contempt sanctions, it is beyond the power of the court to enter the order, and if entered it is completely void. Short of the point of unconstitutionality, however, there is a range of cases in which the clearest order the court is capable of issuing under the circumstances would be unsatisfactory and should therefore be denied as a matter of discretion. Such an order, if entered, would merely be erroneous, and must be obeyed to the best of the respondent's ability until reversed on appeal. In the relatively few cases dealing with this principle, it is often difficult to tell from the court's opinion which ground it relies upon—discretion or lack of jurisdiction, and where both grounds are stated, it is always unclear whether the discretionary ground would lead the court to deny the injunction if the constitutional ground were not also present.

The major distinction between this principle and the last principle discussed is that here the practical difficulty lies in *drafting* any adequate order, while there the problem lay in *enforcing* it.

7. HE WHO COMES IN EQUITY MUST COME WITH CLEAN HANDS

The principle that "he who comes into equity must come with clean hands" is consistent with the nature of a court that functions to administer fairness and justice, rather than rigid rules of law. It allows the equity court, in its discretion, to withhold any remedy from a petitioner who has himself been guilty of some unfairness or injustice in regard to the subject matter of his petition. The principle is not applied for the protection of the respondent, but rather for the protection of the interests of the court itself. It allows the court of equity to avoid being placed in the compromising position of using the powers entrusted to it to aid a petitioner in accomplishing

[*97*]

an unjust result. It has been well summarized as follows:

> "A court of equity acts only when and as conscience commands, and if the conduct of the plaintiff be offensive to the dictates of natural justice, then, whatever may be the rights he possesses and whatever use he may make of them in a court of law, he will be held remediless in a court of equity."

Deweese v. Reinhard, 165 U.S. 386 (1897).

For example, in Morton Salt Co. v. G. S. Suppiger Co., 314 U.S. 488 (1942), the petitioner sought an injunction against infringement of its patent on a machine for depositing salt tablets in food being canned. The court found that the petitioner was using its patent monopoly to violate the anti-trust laws by requiring licensees to use only its own unpatented salt tablets, and for that reason, the court denied any relief.

Since the "clean hands" principle is applied, not as a protection for the respondent, but rather as a disability of the petitioner in protection of the court's interests, it can be brought to the attention of the court in any way. It can be raised by the respondent at any time during the trial, whether he has pleaded the issue or not, and whether he is himself guilty of equal or greater injustice or not. In fact, the respondent cannot waive the right to raise the issue. It is not even necessary that the respondent have personally suffered harm from the petitioner's misconduct. It also follows that the court can raise the issue *sua sponte* at any time that the matter comes to its attention. The one limitation imposed by most courts is that the issue of unclean hands must arise, if at all, before the trial court, so that that court may pass on it, and the person against whom it applies may offer any evidence that would bear on the issue. See, Fibreboard Paper Prod. Corp. v. East Bay Union of Machinists, 227 Cal.App.2d 675, 39 Cal.Rptr. 64 (1964).

Since this principle is one of broad discretion, the types of misconduct that will lead to its application are difficult to define. It is clear, however, that the misconduct need not be either criminal or the basis for any legal action. The principle will generally be triggered by conduct amounting to bad faith, deception, fraud, or injustice. For example, in Carmen v. Fox Film Corp., 269 F. 928 (2d Cir. 1920), the petitioner signed a contract to perform as an actress for the Fox Film Company while she was still a minor. She later signed a conflicting contract to perform for the Frank A. Keeney Pictures Corp., repudiating her contract with Fox when she reached majority. Fox and Keeney reached an agreement between themselves that Keeney would not employ her until the status of their contracts was determined by a court. The petitioner asked the equity court to enjoin Fox from interfering with her contract with Keeney. The court refused to grant her any relief because she had violated her *moral* obligation to abide by her original contract with Fox—even though she was under no *legal* obligation.

Although there is no clear definition of what amounts to "unclean hands," there are several particular circumstances that recur frequently in the cases. They are:

1. Denial of specific performance of a contract because the petitioner obtained the contract unfairly;

2. Denial of an injunction against unfair competition because the good will sought to be protected had been built up by means of false advertising;

3. Denial of an injunction against infringement of a patent because the petitioner had used the patent to violate the anti-trust laws;

4. Denial of an injunction because the petitioner was guilty of a violation of a statute in connection with the subject matter of the petition; and

5. Denial of relief because the petitioner had used false evidence in the course of the proceeding.

One absolute limitation on the principle is that the court will only deny relief for misconduct occurring in the transaction which is the subject matter of the suit. The court does not pass judgment on the general character or past behavior of the petitioner. It is only concerned with the effect of the petitioner's misconduct on the particular transaction before the court. This can be demonstrated by comparing two cases. In Seagirt Realty Corps. v. Chazanoff, 13 N.Y.2d 282, 246 N.Y.S.2d 613, 196 N.E.2d 254 (1963), the petitioner conveyed land without consideration to his son in order to conceal it from creditors. The son agreed to reconvey it on demand. The petitioner went through bankruptcy, in the course of which he swore that he had no interest in realty. Subsequently, the land was reconveyed to him on his request, and he was given a deed which he lost prior to recording it. He brought a bill in equity asking the court to order that he be given a substitute deed. The trial court denied relief on the grounds of unclean hands. The appellate court reversed on the ground that the petitioner's fraud affected only the original conveyance and reconveyance, and was not a part of the current transaction—the execution of a replacement deed. The court noted that "Equity is not an avenger at large."

Compare this case with Pattison v. Pattison, 301 N.Y. 65, 92 N.E.2d 890 (1950), where the petitioner conveyed land to conceal it from creditors and subsequently brought a bill in equity to have the court order reconveyance of the land to him. Here the court denied relief on the grounds of unclean hands because the fraud was an integral part of the transaction before the court.

This principle will apply to preclude relief for any party seeking equitable relief, whether he is the petitioner or a respondent who has filed a cross-bill. The court will not, however, apply the principle to deny relief to a petitioner whose agent has been guilty of misconduct, as long as the petitioner has not authorized or benefited from the agent's misconduct.

Since the court applies this principle as a matter of discretion, it will not blindly deny relief for any misconduct by the petitioner in the way that a court of law would deny recovery for any contributory negligence on the part of a plaintiff. In Republic Molding Corp. v. B. W. Photo Utilities, 319 F.2d 347 (9th Cir. 1963), the petitioner sued to enjoin manufacture of a plastic vegetable bin, similar in shape and design to the petitioner's, on the ground that he had developed a secondary meaning to his design—that is, the public had come to identify vegetable bins of that shape and design as coming from the petitioner. The respondent raised the issue of unclean hands, alleging that the petitioner had developed the secondary meaning by falsely stamping an inscription on his product that a patent application was pending—all in violation of a federal statute.

The court refused to apply the unclean hands doctrine, stating that:

> "the court should not automatically condone the defendant's infractions because the plaintiff is also blameworthy, thereby leaving two wrongs unremedied and increasing the injury to the public. Rather the court must weigh the substance of the right asserted by plaintiff against the transgression which, it is contended, serves to foreclose that right. The relative extent of each party's wrong upon the other and upon the public should be taken into account, and an equitable balance struck."

The court concluded that the harm to the public in allowing the marketing of a product confusingly similar to the petitioner's outweighed the court's interest in denying relief because of the petitioner's alleged misconduct.

In one exceptional case the court struck an interesting compromise. In Hartman v. Cohn, 350 Pa. 41, 38 A.2d 22 (1944), the court granted relief in spite of a finding that the petitioner had been guilty of false advertising, *on condition that* the petitioner immediately stop advertising falsely. This conditional granting of relief is a rare exception to the rule that the court will generally weigh the circumstances and simply grant or deny relief.

Since, in applying the principle, the court is not passing on the merits of the case, but is merely declaring a disability of a petitioner to sue for relief in that court of equity, a dismissal for unclean hands does not bar an action at law on the same claim. In the *Carmen* case, discussed above, the fact that the petitioner could not obtain an injunction against the Fox Film Corp. did not preclude her suing Fox in a legal action. Carmen v. Fox Film Corp., 204 App.Div. 776, 198 N.Y.S. 766 (1927).

8. HE WHO COMES IN EQUITY MUST DO EQUITY

In order to insure that by granting relief the court is not conferring an unjust enrichment on the petitioner at the expense of the respondent, the court can condition relief upon the petitioner's doing whatever is necessary to effect justice between the parties. For example, if the petitioner is asking the court to order the respondent to re-transfer title to land which had been conveyed by the petitioner under duress, fraud, or mistake, the court can condition its order upon the petitioner's returning to the respondent any consideration he has received for the land. The court might also wish to condition relief on the petitioner's paying the respondent for any permanent improvements made on the land by the respondent. The court will only order payment for those improvements, however, which resulted in a benefit to the petitioner.

Another common application of this principle occurs when a petitioner, seeking specific performance of a contract, is required to tender performance of his obligations under the contract as a condition to the court's granting relief. A corollary of this is found in Williams v. Williams, 167 Miss. 115, 148 So. 358 (1933). A divorce decree granted custody of a child to the wife with the stipulation that the child was to visit the husband at reasonable times and intervals. The husband was to pay the wife $40.00 a month in alimony. The wife unreasonably refused to allow the daughter to visit the husband, who then stopped making alimony payments. The wife asked the court to order the husband to pay accrued alimony or be imprisoned for contempt. The court conditioned the granting of this relief on the petitioner's observance of her obligations.

This principle applies only with respect to a party seeking affirmative relief. A respondent who is merely asserting equitable defenses cannot be compelled to act as a condition to asserting the defense. National-Transformer Corp. v. France Mfg. Co., 215 F.2d 343 (6th Cir. 1954). If, however, the *respondent* is asking for *affirmative relief*, the principle does apply.

Under this principle, the petitioner can be compelled to perform acts as a condition to relief that he could not otherwise be ordered to perform. For example, if justice requires it, relief can be conditioned upon the petitioner's making payments on an obligation barred by the statute of limitations. An infant seeking to cancel a contract can be made to do justice to the respondent as a condition to relief. In Parker v. Stephenson, 127 Va. 431, 104 S.E. 39 (1920), for example, a minor inherited a two-thirds interest in land, which was subsequently mortgaged to pay for his support and later sold in foreclosure of the mortgage. The infant petitioned to have the sale set aside because his rights as an "infant" were not protected according to the state statute regulating infant's contracts of sale. The court conditioned relief on return by the minor of two-thirds of the purchase price plus two-thirds payment for any insurance premiums and taxes paid by the buyer, and any improvements made on the land while the buyer was in possession.

One limitation on this principle is that the court can require the petitioner to do equity only in regard to the transaction before the court. If, for example, a petitioner seeks to cancel a debt as usurious, the court can require the petitioner to return the principal and even pay the legal rate of interest, but it cannot require payment of another debt owed by the petitioner to the respondent as a condition of relief. Similarly, the court cannot condition relief on the petitioner's doing

[*106*]

equity to a third party not before the court. For example, if the petitioner owed a fee to the broker who arranged the sale of the petitioner's land, and the petitioner is seeking cancellation of the deed of the land to the respondent, the court cannot condition relief between petitioner and respondent on the petitioner's payment of the fee due to the broker.

Since this principle, unlike the clean hands doctrine, acts for the benefit of the respondent, and not the court, it must be pleaded by the respondent, or it will be considered waived.

9. EQUITY AIDS THE VIGILANT

The doctrine of laches (from the French word for delay) is traditionally summarized by the phrase: Equity aids the vigilant, and not those who slumber on their rights. It is analogous to the effect of a statute of limitations in a court of law. As a matter of fact, the difference between the two is typical of the differences between legal and equitable rules. The statute of limitations at law is clear, precise and unbending. The doctrine of laches is applied at the discretion of the court, weighing the circumstances and equities of the particular case.

There are two elements necessary to the application of the doctrine of laches as a bar to the petitioner's claim. If, (1) The petitioner has *unreasonably* delayed in bringing his action, and (2) this unreasonable delay has caused harm or prejudice to the respondent, the petitioner will not be granted relief. If either element is missing the doctrine will not apply. It is possible, therefore, for the actual time elapsed between the arising of the cause of action and its prosecution by the petitioner to be great without the application of laches because either the delay was reasonable under the circumstances or the respondent suffered no great harm because of it. It is also possible for a short but unreasonable lapse of time to result in laches if it caused some prejudice to the respondent.

The forms of possible prejudice suffered by a respondent are many, but three of the most common are these.

a.   LOSS OF EVIDENCE

In Patton v. Commonwealth Trust Co., 276 Pa. 95, 119 A. 834 (1923), the petitioner delayed bringing his action for fraud for nearly five years after he had discovered it. During that time, the main witness for the respondent had died. The defense of laches was allowed. Other instances of prejudice of this type include loss or destruction of documents or other physical evidence.

b.   CHANGE IN SITUATION

In Gorham v. Sayles, 23 R.I. 449, 50 A. 848 (1901), a vendee bought a factory in 1872 on the top of which was an ancient bell. In the deed, title to the bell was expressly reserved in the vendor. Subsequently the vendee sold the factory to the respondent who assumed that the bell went with it. The original vendor brought a bill more than six years later asking the court to order the respondent to turn over possession of the bell. The court found that during petitioner's delay, the respondent's circumstances had changed. Respondent could no longer bring a legal action against *his* vendor because his claim would be barred by the statute of limitations. For that reason the doctrine of laches was applied.

The possible combinations of changed circumstances are practically limitless. The keynote, however, is a change occurring during the period of the petitioner's unreasonable delay that would make the granting of relief to the petitioner unduly burdensome to the respondent.

c. CHANGE IN VALUE OF SUBJECT MATTER

In Landell v. Northern Pac. Ry. Co., 122 F. Supp. 253 (D.C.D.C.1954), aff'd 223 F.2d 316 (D. C.Cir.1955), during the reorganization of the Northern Pacific Railroad, all of its assets were taken over by a private corporation. Some minority shareholders of the railroad objected to this action for fifty years before bringing an equitable action to set aside the transfer of assets. The defendant pleaded the defense of laches. During that fifty years, track mileage had increased fifty percent. The value of property owned by the railroad had increased from 300 million dollars to 820 million. The lines and equipment of other lines had been acquired, and stock and bond issues had been sold to the public. Because of these changes in the subject matter, the court barred the plaintiff's claim.

The court will pay particular attention to this form of prejudice to the respondent's rights in cases where the plaintiff has delayed his action in order to wait and see whether there would be an increase or decrease in the value of the subject matter. In Groesbeck v. Morgan, 206 N.Y. 385, 99 N.E. 1046 (1912), for example, the vendee in a contract for the sale of land delayed for four years and nine months before bringing his bill for specific performance. During that time he watched the value of the land increase greatly before deciding whether or not to enforce his contract.

In exercising its discretion, the court will also consider the effect of the petitioner's delay on the interests of third parties and the public. In the *Northern Pacific Railway* case cited above, for example, the court was influenced by the reliance that third parties had come to place on the corporate stability of the railroad in investing in its stocks and bonds. The public interest in the railroad as a common carrier was also considered of importance. In Sheldon v. Rockwell, 9 Wis. 166 (1859), the respondent had built a dam in 1937 which had been destroyed by flood five times. The respondent had completely rebuilt it four times and was about to rebuild it a fifth time in 1856 when the petitioner brought a bill to restrain the rebuilding of the dam as a violation of his water rights. The court held the plaintiff's claim barred by laches because of the unreasonable delay of nineteen years, during which time the public had come to rely on the existence of the dam.

In order to avoid a bar to relief because of unreasonable delay, the petitioner is required not only to file the action within a reasonable time but also to prosecute the action with diligence. In Bauby v. Krasow, 107 Conn. 109, 139 A. 508 (1927), for example, the petitioner filed his action promptly, but his failure to ask for a preliminary injunction to restrain the erection of a building defeated his claim for a final injunction to compel removal of the building once built.

Practically without exception, courts of equity will not accept the faulty judgment or advice of petitioner's counsel as a counter-defense to the charge of laches. See Landell v. Northern Pac. Ry. Co., supra.

There are certain instances in which the doctrine of laches will not apply, regardless of the length of time elapsed. It will not apply, for example, in any case in which the petitioner is insane or an infant. Also, if a public official, acting for the state or federal government is guilty of unreasonable delay, this will not bar later assertions of the rights of the government.

The petitioner's claim is also unaffected by delay in cases where the petitioner is led to believe that the respondent does not contest the claim. In fact, laches generally will not apply in any case in which the petitioner's delay had been induced by an action or representation of the respondent.

The doctrine of laches will also not apply in any case in which the plaintiff could not reasonably have been expected to know of the facts which gave rise to his claim. This is particularly true in a case of fraud, where the respondent has concealed the facts from the petitioner. If, however, the petitioner has been aware of the facts but has not pressed his claim because of a mistake of law, laches will apply. It is also no excuse for the petitioner's delay that the respondent was at all times aware of the plaintiff's claim. The respondent is not required to sit and wait for the petitioner to act on his rights at his pleasure.

Where the petitioner is seeking equitable protection for what is actually a legal right, such as

[*112*]

specific enforcement of a contract, equity courts have devised a rule of thumb in regard to the statute of limitations that would apply if the petitioner were suing on his right at law. If, as in most cases, the particular statute of limitations does not apply to equity actions, the court will place the burden of proof on the plaintiff to show that any delay in excess of the period specified by the statute of limitations was reasonable. If, on the other hand, the time elapsed was less than the period of the statute of limitations, the burden is on the respondent to show that it was unreasonable.

Most states now have modern statutes of limitations which expressly include actions in equity and thereby limit the power of the court to grant relief. The doctrine of laches still has a part to play, however, in that the court can hold that a delay in bringing the action, shorter than the period of the statute of limitations, is nevertheless unreasonable and bars the petitioner's action.

10. STANDING

There are certain situations in which a court of equity will deny relief regardless of the merits of the case because the petitioner is deemed to lack standing to bring the action. It is generally the rule that unless the respondent raises the issue affirmatively, it is considered waived. There are many situations in which the issue can arise, but the following are among the most common in courts of equity.

a.   PRIVATE INDIVIDUAL SUING TO ENJOIN A PUBLIC NUISANCE

The principle of lack of standing is commonly applied when a private individual seeks to enjoin a public nuisance. The principle has developed that unless the petitioner can show that he suffers an injury different in kind, rather than merely in degree, from that suffered by the rest of the public affected by the nuisance, he has no standing to bring the action. Only the appropriate public official, such as an attorney general or a district attorney had standing to prosecute the action. Compare two cases in this respect. In Livingston v. Cunningham, 188 Iowa 254, 175 N. W. 980 (1920), the petitioner claimed that a stretch of road was a public highway and sued to enjoin the respondent from continuing to fence off a portion of it as his own private property. The petitioner claimed that he was damaged in that (a) he was unable to haul ice out of a certain lake by the most direct route in the course of his business, and (b) the blockading of the roadway made it more difficult for patrons to reach his ice-cream parlor. The court held that the *inconvenience* suffered by the petitioner was similar to that suffered by the public generally and differed only in degree. Relief was denied for lack of standing. In Gulf States Steel Co. v. Beveridge, 209 Ala. 473, 96 So. 587 (1923), a taxi driver brought suit to enjoin the blocking of a road, alleging that it made it *impossible* for him to get his passengers to their destinations. In this case the court held that the damage suffered by the petitioner, the *impossibility* of performing the functions of his occupation, differed in kind from the general *inconvenience* suffered by the public, and therefore the petitioner had standing to bring action against the public nuisance.

The reason for the principle here is that without the requirement of an interest in the petitioner different in kind from that of the general public, individual petitioners could bring innumerable suits involving great expense and harassment to the respondent, and a decree in favor of the respondent in one action would not bar suit by other petitioners. For this reason, absent a special kind of damage, standing is reserved to the attorney general or district attorney representing the public.

b. ACTIONS BASED ON A STATUTE

A private citizen does not have standing to bring an action to enjoin a business competitor from engaging in competition in violation of a restricting or licensing statute unless one purpose of the statute is clearly to protect competitors. In Massachusetts Society of Optometrists v. Waddick, 340 Mass. 581, 165 N.E.2d 394 (1960), a registered optometrist sought an injunction against the respondent's continuing to practice optometry without a license in violation of the state licensing statute. The court dismissed the action for lack of standing since the purpose of the licensing statute was not to protect competing optometrists, but rather to protect the public from untrained optometrists. Only the District Attorney or the Attorney General would have standing to bring action under the statute.

c. TAX PAYER SUITS

A third common category in which the doctrine of lack of standing is applied is that of suits by taxpayers to enjoin the improper spending of tax revenue by the government. The basic question on the issue of standing here is whether or not the taxpayer has a sufficient personal interest in the public fund to be allowed standing. As a general rule of thumb it has been held that a taxpayer does have standing to bring such an action at the municipal level because of the relative proportion of his contribution to the fund and the immediacy of his interest in municipal activity. It is also generally held that a taxpayer does not have standing to contest the expenditure of public funds at the state level because of the diminished proportion of his contribution. Until the case of Flast v. Cohen, 392 U.S. 83 (1968), it had been consistently held since Frothingham v. Mellon, 262 U.S. 447 (1923), that a taxpayer had no standing to challenge the expenditure of federal funds. In Flast v. Cohen, however, the Court abandoned any universal, across-the-board principle that taxpayers in every case lack standing to challenge federal expenditures of tax monies. It substituted a rule of case-by-case analysis, whereby the individual taxpayer is to be given the opportunity to establish in any given case that he has a sufficient stake in the outcome of the substantive issues to be a proper party to litigate those issues. The court broke the issue of standing in this context into two elements. The taxpayer must demonstrate first that there is a logical connection between his status and the legislation being attacked. A person suing in the capacity of *taxpayer*, for example, would have standing to challenge federal legislation specifically exercising the *taxing and spending* power of Congress under Article 1, section 8 of the Constitution; but would not have standing to challenge, for example, a piece of regulatory legislation under the Commerce Clause, even though some incidental use of the taxing or spending power might be incidental to it. Secondly, the petitioner must establish a clear connection between his status as taxpayer and the precise nature of the constitutional violation which he is attacking. In the *Flast* case, the petitioner sought to enjoin expenditure of federal funds in aid of private schools as a violation of the Establishment and Free Exercise of Religion clauses of the First Amendment. The court held that the first element of standing was satisfied because the legislation was an exercise of Article 1, section 8 power to spend for the general welfare and involved a substantial expenditure of federal tax funds. The second requirement was met because history indicated that one specific evil attempted to be avoided by the Establishment and Free Exercise Clauses of the First Amendment was the spending of federal tax monies to favor one religion over another, and therefore a taxpayer would be a reasonable party to sue to enforce these provisions.

With this limited exception covered by the *Flast* case, the general rule remains that in most instances a taxpayer will be found to lack standing to challenge federal expenditures.

11.   ABSTENTION

Certain types of cases give rise to a conflict over which court or authority is most suited to render a binding decision. Principles have evolved in these areas whereby particular courts, recognizing the appropriateness of leaving the decision to another court or authority, will voluntarily abstain from rendering any decision and will dismiss the action without passing on the merits.

a. FEDERAL COURTS v. STATE COURTS

One example of a court's abstaining out of deference to *another court* occurs when a federal court abstains from a case involving primarily issues of state law. The Supreme Court has always taken the view that "Few public interests have a higher claim upon the discretion of a federal chancellor than the avoidance of needless friction with state policies. . . ." Railroad Comm. of Texas v. Pullman Co., 312 U.S. 496 (1941). Absent a showing that available state procedures are inadequate to enable the petitioner to secure a definitive ruling in the state courts with full protection of his federal rights, federal courts will abstain to allow state courts to interpret matters of state law, out of "scrupulous regard for the rightful independence of the state governments".

By deferring to the state courts on state law issues, however, the federal courts do not abdicate their position as primary interpreters of federal law. They merely *postpone* decision of the federal issues until the state issues have been resolved. See England v. Louisiana State Bd. of Medical Examiners, 375 U.S. 411 (1964).

One narrow exception to this principle of abstention was carved out in the case of Dombrowski v. Pfister, 380 U.S. 479 (1965). The petitioners asked the federal court to enjoin criminal prosecution of them by the Louisiana state authorities under the Louisiana Subversive Activities and Communist Control Law. The particular allegations were that the state authorities were threatening prosecutions in bad faith under an unconstitutional statute with no expectation of obtaining convictions for the sole purpose of harassing and discouraging the petitioners in their civil rights activities. The Court granted the injunction, in spite of the policy of abstention; and for some years it was unclear just how broad an exception had been opened up. Finally, in Younger v. Harris, 401 U.S. 37 (1971), the Court made it clear that *Dombrowski* was to be *very* narrowly interpreted, and that federal interference with state criminal proceedings was to be allowed *only* in the unusual case in which prosecutions under an allegedly unconstitutional statute were threatened for *bad faith* purposes with the result that the petitioner would incur great and immediate irreparable injury if the injunction were not granted. The usual inconveniences and effects of having to defend oneself in a criminal action would not amount to such injury.

b. POLITICAL QUESTIONS

The major area in which an equity court will defer to the primary jurisdiction of *another branch* of the government is that of "political questions". The basic characteristic of a political question is that its resolution by the court would lead the court into conflict with one or both of the coordinate branches of government—i. e., the executive or legislative. The doctrine of abstention here is based primarily on observance of the doctrine of separation of powers.

In 1894, the court in Fletcher v. Tuttle, 151 Ill. 41, 37 N.E. 683 (1894), stated the principle in clear-line, doctrinaire terms. *Political* rights consisted in the power to participate, directly or indirectly, in the establishment or management of the government. *Civil* rights were those which had no relation to the establishment, support or management of the government. The rule was simply laid on these premises that courts of equity (as opposed to courts of law) would not interpose to protect rights which were merely political, where no civil or property right was involved.

Much like the withdrawal from a hard-line rule to the principle of deciding each case according to numerous relevant criteria that took place in Flast v. Cohen, supra, in the area of standing, a similar reformation took place here in the land-

mark case of Baker v. Carr, 369 U.S. 186 (1962).
An equity action was brought by petitioners challenging the apportioning of Tennessee's legisla-
tors among the state's 95 counties on grounds of
denial of equal protection under the Fourteenth
Amendment. The Court refused to dismiss the
case, stating that, "the mere fact that the suit
seeks protection of a political right does not mean
it presents a political question." Instead of an
automatic rule, the Court laid down criteria for
the determination in each case of whether or not
deciding the case would interfere with the separation of powers. The criteria are:

1) Has the issue been committed expressly by
the Constitution to a coordinate political
branch of the government?

2) Are there judicially discoverable and man-
ageable standards for deciding the case?

3) Can the case be decided without some initial policy determination of a kind clearly for
nonjudicial discretion?

4) Can the court decide the case independently
without expressing lack of the respect due a
coordinate branch of the government?

5) Is there an unusual need for unquestioning
adherence to a political decision already
made?

6) Is there a potentiality for embarrassment
from multifarious decisions by different

branches of the government on the same question?

Applying these criteria there are certain clear categories of cases in which the equity court will abstain on the grounds of a political question.

1. The broadest area conceded entirely to the executive and legislative (political) branches involves all questions dealing with foreign relations. The fact that foreign policy has been committed constitutionally to these branches, together with the absolute need for a single-voiced statement of this government's positions, demands this absolute approach. Specific issues in this category include the existence and interpretation of treaties, recognition of foreign governments, and recognition of states of war or peace.

2. Equity courts will also refrain from interfering in the administration of the internal affairs of a political party. In O'Brien v. Brown, 409 U.S. 1 (1972), for example, the court was asked to overrule the decision of the Credentials Committee of the 1972 Democratic National Convention in regard to the seating of certain delegates. The Circuit Court rejected the claims of the petitioners *on the merits*. The Supreme Court, however, stayed the judgment of the Circuit Court—in effect opted for abstention—to allow the political processes to function free from judicial supervision.

In Lynch v. Torquato, 343 F.2d 370 (3rd Cir. 1965), the court dismissed the petitioner's challenge to the method of selecting the Democratic County Committee and Chairman. Since the case involved a fight for control of ordinary party affairs, it amounted to a political question. The same result was reached in Democratic-Farmer-Labor State Central Committee v. Holm, 227 Minn. 52, 33 N.W.2d 831 (1948), where the petitioner asked the court to order the secretary of state to reject one certificate of nominees for election as electors of the D–F–L Party and to place on the ballot the names listed on another certificate. The court ruled that, "In factional controversies within the party, where there is no controlling statute or clear right based on statute law, the courts will not assume jurisdiction, but will leave the matter for determination within the party organization. . . . Such a convention is a deliberative body, and unless it acts arbitrarily, oppressively, or fraudulently, its final determination as to candidates, or any other question of which it has jurisdiction, will be followed by the courts."

3. A court of equity will also refrain from exercising jurisdiction over the appointment or removal of public officers. The primary reason here is that this power has generally been vested in the executive branch or an administrative board, with specific forms of action established

for bringing the matter before courts of *common law*, such as mandamus, prohibition, or *quo warranto*. By interjecting injunctive relief, the equity court would not only be interfering with matters entrusted to another branch, but would also be impinging on the jurisdiction of the common law courts. White v. Berry, 171 U.S. 366 (1898).

c. NON-POLITICAL QUESTIONS

When a petitioner claims that a right, *ordinarily protected by courts of equity*, has been violated by some political action, the court will not abstain. For example, the equity court will protect a petitioner's right to vote for governmental officials, Nixon v. Herndon, 273 U.S. 536 (1927), and even his right to vote in primary elections, United States v. Classic, 313 U.S. 299 (1940). The court will also interfere to see that the petitioner's vote is given equal weight, Baker v. Carr, 369 U.S. 186 (1962), and that he is not denied his political rights because of racial discrimination, Smith v. Allwright, 321 U.S. 649 (1944). As long as the claim pressed by the petitioner is one traditionally recognized and protected by equity courts, and relief can be granted without violating the criteria laid down in Baker v. Carr, supra, the mere fact that the respondent has used a political process, such as discriminatory voting regulations, to violate the petitioner's rights will not transform the issue into a "political question" calling for abstention.

CHAPTER IV

DISCRETION IN ISSUANCE OF THE INJUNCTION

A. GENERALLY

In the third phase of its decision to issue or deny an injunction, the court again employs its discretion, but this time from a different point of view. In the second phase, the court decides to open or close the doors of the courthouse to a particular case depending on whether the case falls within the traditional, evolved view of the types of cases an equity court should handle ("Equity jurisdiction"). In the third phase, the court focuses on the facts of the particular case before it and grants or denies relief on the merits of the action depending on its discretionary view of how to achieve the greatest justice between the parties—keeping one eye on the public interest if it is of any concern in the case. The considerations of the court in this third phase can be clearly divided into 3 areas, each of which is to be weighed in the balance in deciding the case:

1. How serious an injury will the petitioner suffer if the injunction is not issued?

2. How serious a detriment will the defendant suffer if the injunction is issued?

[*126*]

3. What effect, if any, will issuance of the injunction have on the public interest?

Each of these considerations deserves a separate analysis.

B. INJURY TO THE PETITIONER IF THE INJUNCTION IS NOT GRANTED

When the court considered the concept of "irreparable injury" in phase two, it was to determine whether or not the petitioner had an *adequate remedy* at law or elsewhere. The purpose was to insure that the equity court would remain within the bounds of its traditional role and not usurp the jurisdiction of the courts of law (thereby depriving the petitioner of his right to a jury trial). In that context, the question admitted of a "yes" or "no" answer. Either the injury was, or it was not, "irreparable," and the bill was dismissed or retained depending on that decision.

In phase three the question of irreparable injury is examined with an entirely different focus. Here the court is measuring the *relative* seriousness of the petitioner's alleged injury in order to weigh it against the detriment to be suffered by the respondent if the injunction is issued. In this context, the court does not attempt to place the injury into one of two categories—reparable or irreparable—but rather judges it on a continuous scale of seriousness.

One other purpose is served by the court's evaluation of the seriousness of petitioner's injury in phase three. By its evaluation, the court is able to screen out cases of minor injury and to recognize and perpetuate the character of injunctive relief as an *unusual* remedy, to be granted only in unusually deserving cases.

The principle was recently restated as follows:

> "There is no power the exercise of which is more delicate, which requires greater caution, deliberation, and sound discretion, or more dangerous in a doubtful case, than the issuing an injunction; it is the strong arm of equity, that never ought to be extended unless to cases of great injury, where courts of law cannot afford an adequate or commensurate remedy in damages. The right must be clear, the injury impending or threatened, so as to be averted only by the protecting preventive process of injunction: but that will not be awarded in doubtful cases, or new ones, not coming within well established principles; for if it issues erroneously, an irreparable injury is inflicted, for which there can be no redress, it being the act of a court, not of the party who prays for it. It will be refused till the courts are satisfied that the

case before them is of a right about to be destroyed, irreparably injured, or great and lasting injury about to be done by an illegal act; in such a case the court owes it to its suitors and its own principles, to administer the only remedy which the law allows to prevent the commission of such act." Detroit News. Pub. Ass'n v. Detroit Typo. Un. No. 18, 471 F.2d 872 (6th Cir. 1972), quoting from Bonaparte v. Camden, C.C.N.J.1830, Fed. Cas.No.1617.

The degree of seriousness to be attached to a particular injury in this phase rests with the pure discretion and judgment of the individual trial judge, subject to review only on the broad standard of "abuse of discretion." There is, therefore, more room for variance in decisions on similar facts in this phase than in either phase one or phase two. There are, however, certain forms of injury that have almost universally been accorded serious consideration by equity courts. The most common of these are the following.

1. INJURIES TO INTERESTS IN LAND

Because of the historical predilections to which American judges are heir, most injuries to interests in land are considered serious. Where the threat is to a petitioner's title, as in Richards v. Dower, 64 Cal. 62, 28 P. 113 (1883), (Injunction issued to prevent construction of a tunnel passing twenty feet below petitioner's property on major grounds that it would, in time, ripen into an easement), the harm is usually considered of supreme consequence. Where the injury is to the physical character of the land or to the petitioner's quiet enjoyment of it, the court will take a less "per se" approach in considering its relative seriousness, but will still give added weight to the fact that the subject of injury is land.

2. INSOLVENCY OF THE RESPONDENT

Where the petitioner seeks to prevent harm before it occurs by having it enjoined, most courts are practical enough to recognize that even though money damages may theoretically be an adequate form of relief, if the respondent is insolvent, there is little hope for actual relief, and any potential judgment for money damages will be discounted in assessing the seriousness of petitioner's harm.

3. MULTIPLICITY OF SUITS

The fact that a petitioner could acquire relief at law only by bringing numerous suits against one party, or by suing numerous parties individually, would be relevant in both phase two and phase three, but in different ways. For phase two, the petitioner would attempt to convince the court simply that the inconvenience occasioned by the necessity of multiple actions at law had passed the point at which the legal remedy should be considered inadequate. In phase three the petitioner would be interested in establishing the specific *degree* of difficulty to be encountered in obtaining relief elsewhere as one measure of the *relative* harm he would suffer without the injunction.

4. MONEY DAMAGES UNMEASURABLE

Just as the court considers the need for multiple legal actions to obtain compensation as an aggravating factor in assessing petitioner's harm, it will also consider the relative difficulty of establishing, by proof in a court of law, the specific dollar value of the injury. The injury becomes more serious as petitioner is less able to prove specific dollar amounts for recovery at law. Again the *relative degree* of his inability to obtain compensation is relevant, while in phase two the court was only concerned with declaring the legal remedy "adequate" or "inadequate."

C. BALANCING HARM TO THE RESPONDENT

1. BALANCING THE EQUITIES

A. GENERALLY

Situations frequently occur in which the harm suffered by the petitioner, although irreparable and serious to him, is actually far less serious than the harm that would be suffered by the respondent in obeying an injunction issued against him. The attitude of courts of equity toward these situations has taken an interesting turn through the years. Originally, courts insisted that equity will not refuse to protect a man in the possession and enjoyment of his property because that right is less valuable to him than the power to destroy it may be to his neighbor or to the public. Evans v. Reading Chemical & Fertilizing Co., 160 Pa. 209, 28 A. 702 (1894). New York courts were particularly adamant in this approach. In Whalen v. Union Bag & Paper Co., 208 N.Y. 1, 101 N.E. 805 (1913), a petitioner sued to enjoin the operation of a pulp mill on the ground that it was polluting the water upstream. The loss to the petitioner from the nuisance amounted to about $100 a year. The pulp mill represented an investment of over one million dollars and employed 400–500 employees. The court nevertheless granted the injunction closing down the mill, stating that, "Although the damage to the plaintiff may be slight as compared with the defendant's expense of abating the condition, that is not a good reason for refusing an injunction." The court made it clear that "Neither courts of equity nor law can be guided by such a rule, for if followed to its logical conclusion it would deprive the poor litigant of his little property by giving it to those already rich."

In the landmark case of Madison v. Ducktown Sulphur, Copper & Iron Co., 113 Tenn. 331, 83 S. W. 658 (1904), however, the petitioner sought to enjoin the respondent's plant because its fumes were damaging the petitioner's crops in the amount of about $1,000.00 a year. Considering that the plant was worth 2 million dollars, and that to close it down would destroy two great mining and manufacturing enterprises of great importance to the state, and would depopulate a large town, the court could not resist "balancing the equities," and denying the injunction.

The New York Court finally picked up this theme and revised its thinking in Boomer v. Atlantic Cement Co., 26 N.Y.2d 219, 309 N.Y.S.2d 312, 257 N.E.2d 870 (1970). A neighboring land owner sought an injunction against a cement factory to eliminate the nuisance of dirt, smoke and vibration. In spite of the fact that the *Whalen* decision had represented the law in New York, the court could not ignore the disparity between

[*133*]

the total damage to the petitioners, and the value of the plant to be shut down, an investment of 45 million dollars (not to mention the interests of the plant's 300 employees). The court granted the injunction only on condition that the respondent failed to pay the full economic loss to the petitioner. Although this relief, in practical terms, amounted to a money judgment, it differed from legal relief in that the petitioner could collect for both past and future damages in the same action.

It has been suggested that the court in the *Whalen* case, in refusing to balance the equities, might have been considering the fact that Whalen was just one of many riparian owners injured by the nuisance, and that the full extent of the harm to all of those injured should be considered. The Court in the *Boomer* case arrived at a different point of view:

> "The nuisance complained of by these plaintiffs may have other public or private consequences, but these particular parties are the only ones who have sought remedies and the judgment proposed will fully redress them."

b.   SPECIAL CONSIDERATIONS

Two serious factors bearing on a court's decision for or against balancing the equities came to light in two important cases. In Welton v. 40

East Oak St. Building Corp., 70 F.2d 377 (7th Cir. 1934), the petitioner asked the court to order the respondent to reconstruct respondent's building in compliance with the city zoning ordinance. The petitioner's interest seemed relatively slight. The unlawful portion of the building reduced the light reaching the petitioner's property by less than 10%. The critical factor, however, which induced the court to refuse to weigh the relative harms and to grant the injunction, was the fact that the defendant had acted in *knowing* defiance of the zoning ordinance, hoping to pressure the court into denying the injunction because the building was a *fait accompli*. The general rule that has descended is that a court of equity will consider the *deliberateness* and bad faith of the respondent's conduct in deciding whether or not to afford him the consideration of balancing the equities.

The second principle works in the opposite direction and arose out of consideration of the aftermath of cases like *Welton*. The offending building in *Welton* was never actually altered, and the suspicion arises that the respondent found it less financially disastrous to buy off the petitioner than to reconstruct the building. The price the petitioner could demand, with the injunction as a club, would be far in excess of the fair value of the petitioner's harm. If, therefore, a court suspects that the petitioner intends to use the injunction, if granted, not to bring about the specific relief he has asked for, but to extort payment in excess of his damages, the court will be more prone to limit the petitioner to money damages.

It could be argued on behalf of the petitioner that it is unfair to limit his recovery to the dollar value of his loss of use or enjoyment of his property. To allow the respondent to unlawfully encroach upon that use or enjoyment by merely paying the petitioner the amount of his loss in effect gives the respondent the power of eminent domain, in arguable violation of the constitutional prohibition against the taking of property for private use. That strict measure of recovery fails to take into account the petitioner's right to *refuse* to "sell" rights to interfere with his property at the price fixed by the court as "fair," and deprives the petitioner of his ability to bargain with the respondent for sale of his rights at whatever price the respondent might ultimately be willing to pay in order to carry on his own encroaching or nuisance-creating activity. This, it could be argued, amounts to denial of the petitioner's property without due process of law.

c. PRACTICAL ADVANTAGES TO RESPONDENT

It is usually to the great practical advantage of the respondent to limit the petitioner to recovery

of his damages at law in these cases. In addition
to the obvious advantage of being able to buy off
the petitioner for the fair value of his injury,
there are other practical advantages. For example, if the petitioner is limited to an action at
law, the respondent will merely be subject to execution on whatever legal judgment is recovered.
If an injunction is issued, however, and the respondent violates it, he can be subject not only to
paying for any damage done to the petitioner but
also to whatever punitive fine or prison sentence
the court might impose by way of criminal contempt. Secondly, in accord with the Holmesian
view of the law, when the consequences of the respondent's conduct are limited to a determinable
money judgment, the respondent can make the
economic choice to give up his activity, or to continue it and simply pay the price. If an injunction is issued, however, the severity of possible
criminal contempt penalties practically eliminates
that freedom of choice.

d. EXCEPTION: CONTRACT CASES

One area in which a court of equity will not
refuse an injunction because of inconvenience to
the respondent is that in which the petitioner is
seeking a court order specifically enforcing a contract. In West Edmond Hunton Line Unit v.
Stanolind Oil and Gas Co., 193 F.2d 818 (10th

Cir. 1951), individual oil well operators entered into a contract to form a "unit" organization to manage, operate, and further develop the entire area of wells. Subsequently, the unit, in its corporate capacity, sought a court order compelling certain individual operators to abide by their contract to turn over their wells for the exclusive use of the unit. If the injunction were granted, it would cost the individual operators up to $104,-000 to comply with the order. If the injunction were not granted, the greatest possible loss to the unit would be less than $6,000. The lower court balanced the equities and denied the injunction on the ground that if it were granted, the injury to the respondents would be too great compared with the benefit, if any, to the petitioner. On appeal, the order was reversed and the injunction was granted. The court stated:

> "the rights of parties are not governed by comparing the pecuniary loss to one party and the benefit to another, where, as here, the rights of the parties are founded in contract and are sufficiently explicit. . . . If the rights and duties of the parties are fixed by contract, it is not the question of convenience or inconvenience, or the comparative amount of damage or injury resulting from the enforcement of the right. It is the specific performance by the court of

that bargain which the parties have made, with their eyes open."

e. EXCEPTION: STATUTES

A second instance in which the equity court will not pause to balance the equities is one in which a statute specifically provides for issuance of an injunction when certain conditions are met. For example, in State by and through Heltzel v. O. K. Transfer Co., 215 Or. 8, 330 P.2d 510 (1958), the respondent was charged with numerous violations of the common carrier tariffs. The statute provided:

> "Whenever it appears to the commissioner that any person is engaged or about to engage in any acts or practices which constitute or will constitute a violation of this chapter, or of any rule, regulation or order issued under this chapter, he may bring an action in the proper circuit court in the State of Oregon to enjoin such acts or practices and to enforce compliance with such chapter, rule, regulation or order. Upon a *proper showing*, a permanent or temporary injunction, decree or restraining order shall be granted without bond."

The court held that both the language and purpose of the statute required the issuance of the injunction once the commissioner had established merely the conditions specified in the act, without proof of irreparable injury or inadequate remedy elsewhere, *and* without consideration of the relative hardships between respondent and petitioner. "In order to justify the granting of an injunction under an express and unrestricted statutory authority, no balancing of equities is necessary."

Almost without exception, this type of statute provides for injunctive relief in aid of a *public interest,* and therefore courts are under a strong impetus to exercise the statutory grant of power according to its broadest interpretation.

2. PROSPECTIVE HARM

In a further attempt to reach a result that is just to the respondent as well as the petitioner, courts of equity draw a sharp distinction between existing injury-producing situations and those which have not yet come into existence. If the petitioner is attempting to have the court enjoin some *future* conduct from which the petitioner anticipates harm, as opposed to stopping or *changing* the respondent's *current* activity, the court imposes a very strict burden of proof on the petitioner. For example, in City of Lynchburg v. Peters, 145 Va. 1, 133 S.E. 674 (1926), the residents of the city sued to enjoin the city council from closing off certain streets and converting the area into a public park and play-ground. The court stated:

> "It is a well-established principle of equity jurisprudence that where a proposed struc-ture, or the use of it, is not a nuisance per se, a court of equity will not grant an injunc-tion against the erection of the structure or the use, merely because it may become a nui-sance. The alleged nuisance must be the necessary result or the court will await the actual results."

In Otto Seidner, Inc. v. Ralston Purina Co., 67 R. I. 436, 24 A.2d 902 (1942), where the petitioner sought to enjoin the building of a coal bin 75′ from its mayonnaise factory, the court denied the injunction on the ground that the petitioner had not proven "by clear and convincing evidence" that the anticipated damage would be "practically certain to result."

The reason for such a strict burden of proof in cases of other than *per se* nuisances such as pros-titution, illegal gambling, or sale of liquor, is that the court is reluctant to deprive the defendant of his right to make lawful use of his property on a mere chance, or even probability, that he will misuse the privilege. Unless the harm feared by the petitioner is provably certain, the court would prefer to leave the respondent's rights unrestrict-ed, the burden being on him to take whatever precautions are necessary to prevent his proposed use of the property from resulting in harm to the petitioner. If he should fail, and the harm actually occurs, the petitioner has recourse to injunctive relief *then,* as well as the money damages for the harm done. The defendant runs the risk of losing the effect of his investment, but equity courts have decided that he should be allowed to take that risk, if he chooses, in order not to unduly restrain his freedom.

D. PUBLIC INTEREST

The third element affecting the discretionary decision of the court in the third stage is the effect of the injunction on the public interest. This effect can occur in either of two ways—directly or indirectly.

1. DIRECTLY

In some cases, an action which seems to be brought on behalf of a private individual, is actually brought for the purpose of directly effectuating a public policy. For example, in Porter v. Warner Holding Co., 328 U.S. 395 (1946), the Office of Price Administration asked the court to enjoin specific violations of the Price Control Act and to order refund by a landlord to the tenants on whose behalf the action was brought. The court interpreted the Act broadly as granting power to the court to enter such a repayment order because, "In framing such remedies under § 205(a), courts must act primarily to effectuate the policy of the Emergency Price Control Act and to protect the public interest while giving necessary respect to the private interests involved."

Similarly, in Wirtz v. Alapaha Yellow Pine Products, Inc., 217 F.Supp. 465 (M.D.Ga.1963), the Secretary of Labor brought an action under the Fair Labor Standards Act, seeking an injunction against violations of the minimum wage laws, and also against the respondent's withholding payment of minimum wages for past services of its employees. The respondent argued that the court lacked the power under the Act to order payment of back wages. The court held for the petitioner, stating that, "since the public interest is involved . . . those equitable powers assume an even broader and more flexible character than when only a private controversy is at stake. . . . Courts of equity may, and frequently do, go much farther both to give and withhold relief in furtherance of the public interest than they are accustomed to go when only private interests are involved."

2. INDIRECTLY

a. GENERALLY

In a number of cases, although the court's primary purpose is not the effectuation of a broad public policy through private action, the court is influenced in weighing the equities between the petitioner and respondent by whatever side effect an injunction will have on the public interest. For example, in Northern Indiana Public Service Co. v. W. J. & M. S. Vesey, 210 Ind. 338, 200 N.E. 620 (1936), the petitioner sought to enjoin operation of the respondent's gas plant because the gases, odors, ammonia and smoke produced by the plant were damaging the near-by greenhouse. The court based its denial of the injunction on the public interest in the operation of the gas plant.

b. POLLUTION

In the area of cases involving pollution, courts of equity must frequently categorize a particular case as falling within one or the other of two categories for purposes of the remedy to be granted. In the first type, the harm caused by the pollution will be considered unreasonable and enjoinable *only* if the respondent refuses to pay the cost of the injury. In this situation, the court will usually deny an injunction and leave the petitioner to his remedy at law; or grant the injunction, but make it conditional upon the respondent's failure to pay for the damages. In the second type, the harm to the petitioner is considered so serious that fair relief cannot be achieved by the payment of money damages, and therefore an injunction is the only adequate remedy. The decision as to whether any particular case falls within the first or second category is one of discretion, and the court will be heavily influenced by the effect on the public interest of granting or withholding an injunction. This influence could weigh in favor of the respondent if the polluting enterprise is necessary to the community, or in favor of the petitioner if a significant segment of the community is affected by the pollution.

In the recent case of Boomer v. Atlantic Cement Co., 26 N.Y.2d 219, 257 N.E.2d 870, 309 N.Y. S.2d 312 (1970), however, the court rejected this approach of allowing the public interest in eliminating pollution to sway the decision in favor of the petitioner. The reasoning could well influence other courts in this area. There the petitioner sought to enjoin operation of a cement plant because of the dirt, smoke and vibration produced by it in spite of its use of the most modern pollution controls. On the issue of the public concern with air pollution, the court stated that:

> "The threshold question raised by the division of view on this appeal is whether the court should resolve the litigation between the parties now before it as equitably as seems possible; or whether, seeking promotion of the general public welfare, it should channel private litigation into broad public objectives. . . . It is a rare exercise of judicial power to use a decision in private litigation as a purposeful mechanism to achieve direct public objectives greatly beyond the rights and interests before the court."

The court decided that since it would probably require massive public, as well as private, expenditures, and also sophisticated interstate controls, to achieve a practical solution to the technical problems of pollution, it would be a misuse of the court's power and grossly inequitable to the respondent to attempt to wage a war against pollution on the tiny battlefield of this case. The court therefore decided the equities simply between the parties, denying the injunction but granting money damages.

c.   FREE SPEECH

In the area of injunctions against free speech the element of public interest is of extreme importance. In some situations, the policy favoring freedom of speech is so strong that practically no demonstration of harm by the petitioner will overcome the court's reluctance to restrain that freedom. This reluctance was touched upon in Chapter III in the discussion of the principle that equity will not enjoin a libel. As a number of courts have stated, the reason for the court's adamance on this point is to preserve the *public benefit* that flows from maintaining a society of free and open communication, and not merely to protect the interest of the private litigant. This is illustrated by the selection of areas in which the court will adamantly refuse an injunction. It is, for example, practically impossible for a petitioner to obtain an injunction restraining publication of a book, newspaper, or other medium of communication in which the public has an interest for informational, educational or even entertainment purposes. The Supreme Court has, in fact, held that the First Amendment prohibits even the awarding of *damages* for defamatory falsehoods against public officials regarding their official conduct in the absence of a showing of willful or reckless disregard for the truth. New York Times Co. v. Sullivan, 376 U.S. 254 (1964). Similarly, in Krebiozen Research Foundations v. Beacon Press, 334 Mass. 86, 134 N.E.2d 1 (1956), the petitioners sought to enjoin publication of a book alleged to contain false and malicious statements in derogation of a new drug developed by the petitioner for the treatment of cancer. The court denied the injunction on the grounds that the establishment of the truth about Krebiozen was a matter of critical importance to the public interest, and that the surest method of arriving at the truth would be to allow full and free discussion on the theory that one man's judgment of falsity is not to be trusted in determining what people should be allowed to read. In view of the public interest, the court preferred to let the petitioner take his chances on recovering money damages at law.

On the other hand, in the area of false advertising, where there is no *major public interest* in the subject matter of the ideas communicated, but rather a primarily economic interest on the part of the private advertiser, courts have shown little reluctance to enter an injunction.

d. PUBLIC INTEREST FAVORING PETITIONER

Occasionally, the public interest element works in favor for the petitioner and leads to the granting of an injunction that might not otherwise have been granted. In Harris Stanley Coal & Land Co. v. Chesapeake & O. Ry. Co., 154 F.2d 450 (6th Cir. 1946), the railroad asked the court to enjoin certain mine owners from digging in such a way as to create a danger of landslide. The court might have denied this injunction on the ground that it involved a *prospective* creation of a nuisance (see discussion of prospective harm above). Nevertheless, the court looked beyond the interests of the petitioner railroad to the interests of the members of the public that would be riding the trains. It granted the injunction, stating that, "It may be that such disaster could occur only upon a concatenation of circumstances of not too great probability, and that the odds are against it. It is common experience, however, that catastrophies occur at unexpected times and in unforeseen places. . . . A court of equity will not gamble with human life, at whatever odds, and for loss of life there is no remedy that in an equitable sense is adequate."

CHAPTER V

TYPES OF INJUNCTIONS

A. GENERAL

Injunctions fall generally into two distinct categories, permanent injunctions and interlocutory injunctions. Permanent injunctions are those issued as complete injunctive relief to the petitioner (so far as this is possible) after a full hearing on the merits of the petition. Interlocutory injunctions are those issued at any time during the pendency of the litigation for the short-term purpose of preventing irreparable injury to the petitioner prior to the time that the court will be in a position to either grant or deny permanent relief on the merits. In accordance with their purpose, interlocutory injunctions are limited in duration to some specified length of time, or at the very outside, to the time of conclusion of the case on the merits. Within the category of interlocutory injunctions there are two distinct types which must be considered individually. The first is generally referred to as a *preliminary injunction,* and includes any interlocutory injunction granted after the respondent has been given notice and the opportunity to participate in a hearing on whether or not that injunction should issue. The second is generally referred to as a *temporary re-*

straining order, and differs from a preliminary
injunction primarily in that it is issued *ex parte*,
with no notice or opportunity to be heard granted
to the respondent. Temporary restraining orders
supply the need for relief in those situations in
which the petitioner will suffer irreparable injury
if relief is not granted *immediately*, and time
simply does not permit either the delivery of notice or the holding of a hearing. Since each of
these types of injunction plays a critical and distinct role in the scheme of equitable relief, the
special characteristics of each type will be discussed separately below.

B. INTERLOCUTORY INJUNCTIONS

1. CHARACTERISTICS COMMON TO ALL INTERLOCUTORY INJUNCTIONS

The two types of interlocutory injunctions, preliminary injunctions and temporary restraining
orders, have a number of characteristics in common. These will be discussed below prior to a
discussion of those characteristics which distinguish them.

a. PURPOSE

The sole legitimate purpose of an interlocutory
injunction, granted, by definition, prior to a full
and complete hearing on the merits of the litiga-

tion, is to prevent a change in circumstances that will irreparably injure the petitioner before the court has time to decide finally on the granting or denying of permanent relief. The usual phrase employed by the courts is that an interlocutory injunction is issued to "hold the status quo between the parties." The "status quo" referred to has been defined as the *last uncontested status* between the parties preceding the pending controversy. Tanner Motor Livery, Ltd. v. Avis, Inc., 316 F.2d 804 (9th Cir. 1963). If, for example, A had for some time owned and occupied property when B appeared claiming ownership of the same property and expressing an intent to alter it, A might bring a bill for declaratory judgment to determine his ownership of the property and also for a permanent injunction against B's interfering with that ownership. A would also seek an interlocutory injunction against B's interference with the property during the pendency of the litigation, and the purpose of such an injunction would be to preserve the status quo between the parties that existed prior to the controversy in litigation, that is, the status of A being in quiet occupancy and enjoyment of the undisturbed property.

Courts have seen this preservation of the status quo as serving two interests. It is primarily in the interest of the petitioner to prevent irreparable harm prior to a decision on the merits. It has also been considered to serve the interests of the court as a means of preventing the respondent from taking action which will in practical effect, disable the court from granting any meaningful relief after trial on the merits.

While the "last uncontested status quo" is relatively easy to define semantically, it can present a perplexing problem in attempting to apply it to a practical situation for two reasons. The first is simply that many cases do not present the simple, clear-cut situation of an easily recognized status quo, suddenly interrupted by a contested attempt to change that situation (As was the case with the simple example stated above). In many of the more complicated fact situations presented, for example, by controversies over the management of corporate affairs that have been fermenting over a long period of time from some indiscernable starting point, it is practically impossible to define and then preserve the situation that existed at some point in time when all of the material elements of the relationship between the parties were "uncontested." Where a perfect definition of that point is impossible, the court must simply do its best to define a "status quo" that should be preserved during the pendency of litigation in order to minimize irreparable injury to either the petitioner or the respondent.

The second cause of difficulty arises in situations in which there is no meaningful, static sta-

tus quo between the parties because of the constantly changing dynamics of their relationships.
A perfect example of this situation exists in the
case of labor disputes. Where both labor and
management are constantly employing tactics to
obtain an advantage in the balance of power, it is
nearly impossible to satisfactorily fix a static status quo for preservation. If, for example, an employer were to obtain an interlocutory injunction
against the union's striking, in alleged violation
of a no-strike clause in the collective bargaining
agreement, the result could be disastrously unfair
to the union. The timing of a strike is frequently
critical in terms of days, sometimes in terms of
hours. If the employer were allowed to defuse
the most important weapon in the union's arsenal
in this way, while he remained free to undermine
the union's bargaining position in more subtle
ways, the result would be grossly unfair to the
union. It is extremely difficult to define and
freeze any status quo in the midst of the dynamic
situation of a labor dispute that would not result
in the unjust favoring of one party or the other.
It requires great perception on the part of the
court to recognize the consequences of what appears on the surface in many cases to be merely a
holding of the status quo. Often the court is required to decide at the interlocutory stage, prior
to having the benefit of full testimony and argu-
ments on the merits, which side is to bear the ir-

reparable injury that will inevitably flow from the granting or withholding of an interlocutory injunction. It is at this stage, perhaps, more than any other, that the wisdom and foresight of the court is put to the test.

b. ELEMENTS CONSIDERED BY THE COURT IN GRANTING AN INTERLOCUTORY INJUNCTION

As is true with any type of injunction, the court's decision to grant or deny an interlocutory injunction can be divided into three phases. The discussion above in regard to phase one, regarding personal and subject matter jurisdiction, applies with equal force to interlocutory injunctions. The only instance in which special treatment is accorded to interlocutory, as opposed to permanent, injunctions is that discussed in United States v. United Mine Workers of America, 330 U.S. 258 (1947). In that case the United States was seeking permanent equitable relief against a strike that threatened to paralyze the country's coal industry at a critical period. The court granted an immediate *ex parte* order, enjoining the threatened strike in order to hold the status quo until the court had an opportunity to decide the major threshold question of whether or not Section 4 of the Norris-LaGuardia Act had deprived the court of subject matter jurisdiction to enjoin a strike. The respondent union took the position that the court lacked subject matter jurisdiction and chose simply to ignore the order and proceed with the strike. The Supreme Court decided that the district court did have subject matter jurisdiction but went on to decide the more interesting question of the effect of a temporary order issued to hold the status quo until a trial court would have time to decide a threshold question of subject matter jurisdiction in the event that it was ultimately decided that the court *lacked* this jurisdiction. The court held that a party who violates an interlocutory injunction under those circumstances *will* be subject to criminal contempt sanctions. This decision gives the equity court the practical power to prevent the respondent's causing irreparable injury before the court has the chance to decide whether or not it has the power to continue. This rule only applies in cases in which there is a bona fide question of subject matter jurisdiction. It does not apply where the court's lack of jurisdiction is obvious, or not subject to reasonable argument. Nor does this rule apply to cases in which the court is found to lack party jurisdiction.

The elements that affect phase two of the court's decision on a permanent injunction (see Chapter III above) equally affect the court's decision on an interlocutory injunction. The principles discussed in Chapter III above, such as that equity will not enjoin a crime, or that equity will not issue an injunction where there is an adequate remedy elsewhere, apply equally to all forms of injunctions. Since, however, the purpose of an interlocutory injunction differs from the purpose of a permanent injunction, in that the former seeks only to retain the status quo pending the court's decision on the merits, the court must consider whether or not the remedy at law or elsewhere is adequate to accomplish *that* particular purpose, rather than the more broad purpose of affording permanent relief for the petitioner's problem. Similarly, the short-term nature of the interlocutory injunction may affect the court's decision on whether or not to temporarily enjoin an act which is criminal in nature. The interference with the criminal process is more limited in this case because of the short duration of the injunction.

Since an interlocutory injunction serves not only to protect the petitioner from short-term irreparable injury, but also to aid the court in preventing the respondent from taking any action which will place it beyond the court's practical power to grant meaningful preventive relief to the petitioner, the court will be more inclined to see its way around the principles of phase two that might give it pause in issuing a permanent injunction for the petitioner.

In phase three of its decision on an interlocutory injunction, the court focuses on four particular elements. Here, as in the case of a permanent injunction, the court is dealing in the broad realm of discretion. The four elements are as follows.

(i) *Proof or Irreparable Harm to Petitioner*

The focus of the court's inquiry here is on the seriousness of the harm the petitioner will suffer prior to the time of entry of the final decree in the litigation. The court considers the degree of petitioner's need for an injunction that will hold matters in the last uncontested status quo, as opposed to his need for affirmative permanent relief.

(ii) *Absence of Substantial Counter-Balancing Harm to the Respondent*

The "balancing of the equities" concept plays a much more critical role in the decision on an interlocutory decree than in the decision on a permanent injunction. While the court is less concerned with the problems of adequacy of remedy at law, or interference with the criminal process, because of the shorter duration of the interlocutory decree, it is *more* concerned with any resultant harm to be caused to the respondent by its temporary injunction. There are several reasons for the court's hesitance to deal in any way cavalierly with the respondent's interests at this stage of litigation. For one thing, to be effective, the interlocutory order must be issued within a relatively short space of time after the initial pleading in the case has been filed. This, in many cases, allows the respondent a dangerously short period of time within which to prepare his defenses to the interlocutory injunction. He is often hard-pressed to foresee and communicate to the court all of the adverse ramifications of an interlocutory order. Secondly, the court is well aware that in a situation calling for the court's keenest understanding of frequently complex and conflicting interests, it must enter an order that may have the most serious consequences for one of the two parties on a very truncated explication of the facts, and often hurried analysis of the law. For these reasons, courts are more prone to balance the interests of petitioners and respondents equally in considering temporary relief. The general formula was stated in Texas Pipeline Co. v. Burton Drilling Co., 54 S.W.2d 190 (Tex.Civ.App. 1932):

> "In a doubtful case, where the granting of the injunction would, on the assumption that the defendant ultimately will prevail, cause greater detriment to him than would, on the contrary assumption, be suffered by the complainant, through its refusal, the injunction usually should be denied. But where, in a doubtful case, the denial of the injunction would, on the assumption that the complain-

ant ultimately will prevail, result in greater detriment to him than would, on the contrary assumption, be sustained by the defendant through its allowance, the injunction usually should be granted. The balance of convenience or hardship ordinarily is a factor of controlling importance in cases of substantial doubt existing at the time of granting or refusing the preliminary injunction. Such a doubt may relate either to the facts or to the law of the case, or to both."

What this rather complex formula boils down to is simply that in the preliminary stage, the petitioner's and respondent's interests should be equally balanced. "When the questions to be ultimately decided are serious and doubtful, the legal discretion of the judge should be influenced largely by the balance of equities between the parties. The court should ascertain which of them will suffer the greater detriment or inconvenience by its action. In fact, the balance of convenience or hardship is ordinarily a factor of controlling importance in cases of substantial doubt existing at the time of the granting or refusing of the preliminary injunction." Texas Pipeline Co. v. Burton Drilling Co., supra.

(*iii*) *Absence of Harm to the Public Interest*

This factor plays a role similar to that played in the decision on a permanent injunction. It may be that the public shares a strong interest in preserving the status quo until the rights of the parties to the litigation can be determined, as in the case of United States v. United Mine Workers, 330 U.S. 258 (1947), where the country's interest in maintaining a supply of coal in war-time presented a serious consideration. It may also be that the public interest is diminished because of the short duration of an interlocutory order.

(*iv*) *Likelihood that the Petitioner Will Prevail on the Merits*

Before the court will, on an incomplete presentation of evidence and a quickly prepared briefing of the law, interfere with the liberties of the respondent, the court will require some measure of assurance that the petitioner has a case on which it is likely to prevail on the merits. At the very least, the court will require that the petitioner have stated a *prima facie* case for permanent relief in his petition. W. A. Mack, Inc. v. General Motors Corp., 260 F.2d 886 (7th Cir. 1958). Generally speaking, the greater the imposition on the respondent, requested by way of a petition for an interlocutory order, the greater the court will inquire into the probability of success of the peti-

[*161*]

tioner on the merits after final hearing. The petitioner need not, however, prove his case on the merits in order to obtain an interlocutory injunction. As was stated in B. W. Photo Utilities v. Republic Molding Corp., 280 F.2d 806 (9th Cir. 1960), "It is not the function of a preliminary injunction to decide the case on the merits, and the possibility that the party obtaining a preliminary injunction may not win on the merits at the trial is not determinative of the propriety or validity of the trial court's granting the preliminary injunction."

It is generally conceded by the courts, that in application of the four elements listed above in the discretionary phase of the court's decision, the standards for issuing a preliminary injunction are more demanding than those governing issuance of a permanent injunction. Henson v. Hoth, 258 F.Supp. 33 (D.Colo.1966). This is so because the court is aware of the strictures placed on its decisional process by the necessity for speed, and it is concerned about the potential danger of a rashly issued temporary injunction.

c.   MANDATORY VERSUS PROHIBITORY INTERLOCUTORY INJUNCTIONS

For purposes of inquiring into the propriety of an interlocutory injunction, courts of equity have created the two categories of *mandatory* and *pro-*

[*162*]

hibitory injunctions. The choice of terms is unfortunate in that they can be misleading. The words are used in a highly specific sense to serve a particular function. As will be seen, the term, "prohibitory," does not necessarily refer to an injunction negative in form. Nor does the term "mandatory" necessarily refer to an affirmative order to take action. The specific meaning of the terms is simply this. A prohibitory interlocutory injunction is one that orders the respondent to accomplish whatever is necessary by way of affirmative or negative action *to retain a particular status quo* between the parties. A mandatory interlocutory injunction is one which orders the respondent to take either negative or affirmative action which will *alter* the status quo. As a general rule, since the purpose of an interlocutory injunction is solely to retain the status quo, only a prohibitory injunction is proper. With one exception to be noted below, if an interlocutory injunction is issued which is mandatory in effect, it will be considered erroneous, and will be subject to a motion to vacate before the trial court, or subject to reversal on appeal.

Whether a prohibitory injunction is to be affirmative or negative in form depends upon the particular status quo it is intended to preserve. If the status quo is one of rest or inaction between the parties, the injunction will be negative to retain that state of rest. For example, if A is

[*163*]

in quiet ownership and possession of a piece of property at a time when B claims ownership in himself and threatens to alter the property, such as by cutting down timber, A might bring an action to quiet title, and request an interlocutory injunction against B's disturbing the property prior to trial on the merits. Since the last uncontested status quo between the parties was one in which A was in quiet possession of the property, it was one of rest; and the appropriate prohibitory injunction would be negative in form, ordering B to refrain from interfering with A's quiet possession of the property. If, on the other hand, the last uncontested status quo were one of *action* between the parties, the petitioner might be irreparably injured by an interruption of that action prior to a determination on the merits of whether or not the respondent has the right to interrupt that action. In that case, the proper prohibitory injunction would be affirmative in form, ordering the respondent to continue his prior activities. In Whiteman v. Fuel Gas Co., 139 Pa.St. 492, 20 A. 1062 (1891), the petitioner acceded to the respondent's inducement to build his flint-glass factory in such a way as to be adapted to the use of natural gas for fuel. Once the factory was built, it could not be adapted to any other form of fuel. It was essential to the plaintiff to receive a constant supply of gas, since the glass in the process of being manufactured would crack if there were an interruption of heat. The respondent had contracted to supply a continuous flow of gas fuel and had performed that contract for a period of time when it suddenly decided to shut off the supply of gas. The petitioner claimed that the respondent was in breach of its contract, and brought a petition for a permanent order that the respondent perform according to the terms of its contract. The petitioner also sought an immediate interlocutory injunction to prevent irreparable injury to the glass in the process of being manufactured. The last uncontested status quo between the parties consisted of the respondent's actively supplying gas fuel to the petitioner. In order to continue that status quo in existence, the court ordered the respondent to continue supplying fuel to the petitioner. Although the injunction ordered affirmative action on the part of the respondent, it was "prohibitory" in that it preserved the relevant status quo.

One other situation in which an affirmative order is required to retain the status quo is that which occurred in Keys v. Alligood, 178 N.C. 16, 100 S.E. 113 (1919). There the court issued a preliminary injunction ordering the respondents not to interfere with a certain roadway pending litigation. The respondents were notified of the order and willfully violated it by removing a ditch bank. At the petitioner's request, the court ordered the respondents to take affirmative action to restore the ditch bank to its condition at the time they received notice of the interlocutory injunction. On appeal, the interlocutory injunction was upheld, the court stating, "when one who has notice that an injunction has been granted against him, though he has not been formally served with the writ, does an act which is a violation of the injunction, and thus changes the status of the property involved in the case, the judge may at an interlocutory hearing, or upon an application for an attachment for contempt, require the offender to restore the status as it existed at the time he first received notice that the injunction had been granted."

There is one exception to the general rule that only a prohibitory interlocutory injunction is proper. In the case of Trautwein v. Moreno Mutual Irrigation Co., 22 F.2d 374 (9th Cir. 1927), the respondents were the owners of a system of pipelines used for delivering water for irrigation to neighboring farms for a fee. The petitioners had delivered a quantity of water into the pipelines of the respondent for delivery without previously asking the respondent's permission. The respondent refused to allow the water to be delivered at the other end of the pipelines, simply for the purpose of contesting its legal status as a common carrier. It claimed the status of a private contractor, legally capable of refusing service to any prospective customer. The petitioner brought a bill in equity to test the question of respondent's status and asked for an immediate interlocutory injunction ordering the respondent to deliver the water already placed in the pipelines. The last uncontested status quo between the parties was one of rest, prior to the time the petitioners had delivered water into the pipelines. The interlocutory injunction sought would require affirmative action on the part of the respondent. This would alter that status quo and clearly render the interlocutory injunction mandatory. On appeal, the Ninth Circuit affirmed issuance of the interlocutory injunction. In analyzing the situation in practical terms, it found, a) that if the interlocutory injunction were not issued, the petitioner would suffer *severe* irreparable injury in potential loss of crops, and b) that the respondent would suffer no recognizable injury from such an injunction since the delivery of the water would in no way injure or affect the pipelines nor deprive the respondent of its ability to serve other customers, and the respondent would receive fair compensation for the service, and 3) that a preliminary analysis of the case indicated that the petitioner stood an excellent chance of success on the merits of the litigation. Under these rather rigid circumstances—serious irreparable injury to the petitioner if the injunction is not granted, no substantial injury to the respondent if the injunction is granted, and predictably good chances of success on the final decree by the petitioner—a mandatory interlocutory injunction could properly be issued. This exception is particularly appropriate in cases in which the acts of the respondent complained of are willful or fraudulent or without any sense of justification.

In order to protect a respondent against irreparable injury from an improperly issued mandatory interlocutory injunction before he has the opportunity to have it reversed on appeal, the general rule has evolved that a *mandatory* interlocutory injunction is automatically stayed from the time the respondent takes an appeal of that order until the appellate court has an opportunity to act on the appeal. During that stay, the respondent is under no obligation to obey the injunction. As a practical matter, a respondent should keep it in mind that any willful action during the period of that stay to deliberately thwart the ability of the court to grant meaningful relief to the petitioner could subsequently weigh against him when the court is considering his good faith in the matter in balancing the equities. Short of this practical situation, however, during the pendency of the stay, the respondent will not be subject to contempt sanctions for violating the injunction. The other half of this general rule is that a *prohibitory* interlocutory injunction is *not* automatically stayed on appeal. If the respondent desires immediate relief from the effect of the interlocutory injunction while his appeal is being decided, he must petition the appellate court before whom his appeal is pending for a temporary stay.

While the rule is simple enough to state, its application to particular complex fact situations can be uncomfortably cloudy. The number of dissenting opinions in cases determining that a particular interlocutory injunction is either mandatory or prohibitory indicates the uncertainty to which a respondent can be subject in trying to decide whether or not the interlocutory injunction is, or is not, stayed on appeal. In many cases, he cannot know in advance of the appellate court's decision on the mandatory/prohibitory nature of the injunction whether or not it was stayed during the pendency of the appeal. Needless to say, this leaves him in serious doubt as to whether or not his actions during the time of appeal will subject him to contempt proceedings. In Paramount Pictures Corp. v. Davis, 228 Cal. App.2d 827, 39 Cal.Rptr. 791 (1964), the respondent, Bette Davis, was under contract to perform the role of "Mrs. Hayden" in the making of the motion picture "Where Love Has Gone." The term of her services was expressed in the contract in unclear language, and at a time when she alleged that she believed her obligation for exclusive service to the petitioner was over, she entered into an exclusive service contract with another motion picture company. The petitioner contended that she had further obligations under the first contract and obtained a preliminary injunction preventing her from performing services on the second contract until the court could finally determine her status as a free agent under the first contract. The respondent appealed this temporary injunction and sought a stay of its effect during the pendency of the appeal. This raised the question of whether the temporary injunction was mandatory or prohibitory for purposes of deciding whether or not it was automatically stayed on appeal. The majority of the appellate court interpreted the last uncontested status quo in such a way that it would be altered by performance of the preliminary injunction, and therefore decided that the preliminary injunction was mandatory. The dissent took a different view of the relevant status quo, and concluded that it would be simply preserved by the temporary injunction, thereby determining that the injunction was prohibitory. This type of disagreement among judges is common in situations presenting any but the clearest relevant status quo, and it points up the precarious position of a respondent in deciding whether or not he is free to disregard an interlocutory injunction during the pendency of an appeal.

d. CONDITIONS IMPOSED UPON THE GRANTING OF INTERLOCUTORY INJUNCTIONS

One method employed by the courts to strike a fair balance between the interests of the petitioner and the respondent, short of denying an interlocutory injunction, is to impose conditions on the petitioner. For example, in United States Air Conditioning Corp. v. Fogel, 272 F.2d 879 (3rd Cir. 1959), in a dispute between a tenant and landlord, the tenant sought a preliminary injunction against the landlord's accelerating his rent under the provisions of the lease. The court granted the preliminary injunction *on condition* that the tenant pay his monthly rent plus interest into the court as holder for the protection of the landlord. Similarly, in Long Island R. Co. v. System Federation No. 156, Am. Federation of Labor, 289 F.Supp. 119 (D.C.N.Y.1968), the court granted a preliminary injunction against a work slow-down by the union on condition that the petitioner railroad would not put a three-shift, seven-day operation into effect until all procedures under the Railway Labor Act had been completed.

e. EVIDENCE ON INTERLOCUTORY INJUNCTIONS

Because of the strictures of time implicit in a decision on an interlocutory injunction, courts have made certain accommodations in regard to the usual rules of evidence. For example, affidavits and verified pleadings may be accepted as evidence in spite of the usual hearsay rules. Hunter v. Atchison, T. & S. F. Ry. Co., 188 F.2d 294 (7th Cir. 1951). A number of states have provided by statute that a preliminary injunction may be granted on the basis of the face of the complaint, as long as the complaint is verified by the petitioner himself.

f. BOND

The ability of the court, in its discretion, to impose conditions upon the issuance of interlocutory injunctions was the origin of the power to require the petitioner to undertake to compensate the respondent for damages resulting from an interlocutory injunction later found to have been issued erroneously. This is usually accomplished by requiring the petitioner to file a bond with the court, indemnifying the respondent against such damages. Without such an undertaking, the petitioner could only be held liable at common law for damages resulting from his intentional and malicious obtaining of an erroneous decree. The purpose of the bond is to insure accountability of the petitioner for damages resulting to the respondent from an erroneous injunction obtained through no fault or malice on the part of the petitioner. This is a departure from the usual American practice of not imposing costs on an unsuccessful litigant who has acted in good faith.

The bond serves a number of purposes. It protects the court against being placed in the position of having to choose between the equally unsatisfactory courses of 1) denying the interlocutory injunction, with consequent irreparable injury to the petitioner, in order to prevent serious damage to the respondent, or 2) simply granting the injunction in a doubtful situation in which the court might be erroneously visiting serious harm on the respondent. By means of a bond, the court can insure itself, as far as possible, that an error on its part will injure neither party.

The bond serves the additional purpose of protecting the respondent in a situation in which the law would provide no other cause of action against a petitioner who has acted in good faith.

The bond also works both for and against the petitioner. It not only discourages him from making false or fraudulent claims for interlocutory relief, but also forces him to exercise the greatest caution to see that the court does not issue an injunction at his request that will later be found to have been erroneous. The bond works for him in enabling him to obtain interlocutory relief that might otherwise be denied by the court out of concern for the damage that might be caused to the respondent.

Most states now have a statutory requirement that a bond be imposed as a condition to the granting of an interlocutory injunction. In the federal courts, Rule 65(c) of the Federal Rules of Civil Procedure states in part, "No restraining order or preliminary injunction shall issue except upon the giving of security by the applicant, in such sum as the court deems proper, for the payment of such costs and damages as may be incurred or suffered by any party who is found to have been wrongfully enjoined or restrained."

The usual procedure, even where the bond is statutorily required, is for the judge to fix the amount of the bond in his discretion, depending on his evaluation of the potential harm the respondent is likely to suffer from the interlocutory injunction. Since most state statutes, like Rule 65(c), leave the amount of the bond to the judges' discretion, it is generally agreed that under appropriate circumstances the court can fix the amount at zero, and thereby dispense with the bond. Board of Supervisors of La. St. Univ. & A. & M. College v. Ludley, 252 F.2d 372 (5th Cir. 1958). The circumstances under which the court may appropriately dispense with the bond include:

    a)   Where the petitioner is an indigent, and the respondent is a large institution, so that the potential damage to the respondent is far less significant to it than the burden of posting a bond would be to the petitioner (this assumes good faith on the part of the petitioner);

b) Where there is no proof of the likelihood of harm or loss to the respondent;

c) Where the interlocutory injunction is issued to aid or preserve its jurisdiction over the subject matter involved; and

d) Where the court issues an interlocutory injunction to protect and enforce its lawful orders.

Bivins v. Board of Pub. Ed. & Orphanage for Bibb County, 284 F.Supp. 888 (M.D.Ga.1967).

Except where a common law action will lie for malicious prosecution, the respondent must rely on the bond for recovery. In absence of a bond, no damages may be recovered for the issuance of an interlocutory injunction, "even though it may have been granted without just cause." Benz v. Compania Naviera Hidalgo, 205 F.2d 944 (9th Cir. 1953). Nor can the respondent recover in excess of the upper limits of the bond. This rule is generally followed in state courts, except for the few states in which the simple erroneous requesting of a temporary injunction is a tort.

Since recovery on a bond is analogous to a contract action, the respondent can only recover the dollar amount in damages that he is able to prove. It is possible that the respondent, like the petitioner, could suffer damages not measurable in terms of a specific amount of money. He would, in this case, be unable to recover on the bond. In Ballmer v. Smith, 158 Neb. 495, 63 N. W.2d 862 (1954), a preliminary injunction issued, enjoining the respondent from restoring a stream to its position prior to a flood. By the time the injunction was dissolved, he had lost two years' crops. The court held that he could not recover on the bond because the amount of the damage was too speculative. This possibility of uncompensable harm to the respondent should be considered by the court before issuing an interlocutory injunction. The court could, in many cases, obviate the difficulty by ordering that a liquidated damages clause be included in the bond.

One final limitation on recovery under a bond that should be noted is that recovery can only be had for damages directly resulting from the specific interlocutory order, accruing between the time of its issuance and the time it is declared erroneous.

g. ORDERS MODIFYING OR VACATING AN INTERLOCUTORY INJUNCTION

The trial court that issues an interlocutory injunction retains the power, while the order is outstanding (unless the matter has been removed to the appellate court), to modify or dissolve the order in accordance with its own discretion. Courts have stated, however, that "such modification or dissolution requires a showing of changed circumstances so that continuance of the injunction is no longer justified and/or because it will work oppressively against the enjoined parties. . . . In the absence of such a showing, the injunction will not be disturbed." American Optical Co. v. Rayex Corp., 291 F.Supp. 502 (S.D.N. Y.1967). "An injunction may not be dissolved or modified in the absence of a showing of unforeseeable changes in conditions which have created an exceptional situation." Aaron v. Cooper, 163 F.Supp. 13 (D.C.Ark.1958), reversed on other grounds 257 F.2d 33. Only those parties to the action who are bound by the interlocutory injunction have standing to move to modify or to vacate it.

h. APPEAL OF AN INTERLOCUTORY INJUNCTION

The usual rule in both state and federal courts is that an interlocutory order is not appealable. In the case of an interlocutory injunction, a special exception is made. Under 28 U.S.C.A. §

1292(A), federal courts of appeals have jurisdiction of appeals from:

> "(1) Interlocutory orders of the district courts of the United States . . . granting, continuing, modifying, refusing or dissolving injunctions, or refusing to dissolve or modify injunctions. . . ."

Federal courts have interpreted § 1292(A) as granting power to review *immediately* an order either granting or denying an interlocutory injunction. The reason for this exception is that "If the grant or denial of a preliminary injunction was reviewable only after a "final decision" had been entered below it would frequently be too late for the courts of appeals to undo the harm caused by an erroneous ruling below and recreate a state of affairs in which meaningful relief could be granted to the party entitled to prevail." Chappell & Co. v. Frankel, 367 F.2d 197 (2d Cir. 1966).

The respondent is generally required to abide by the usual rules of procedure for preserving his objections to an order. For example, if, after notice, he has failed to appear to contest the granting of a preliminary injunction, he is deemed to have waived any objection based on adequacy of remedy at law, lack of irreparable injury, and other such non-jurisdictional objections. Similarly, if he has appeared to contest issuance of the order, but failed to raise any of these objections, he will be deemed to have waived them.

i. RES JUDICATA EFFECT OF AN INTERLOCUTORY INJUNCTION

The res judicata effect of an interlocutory injunction is quite limited. As stated in Bursten v. Phillips, 351 F.2d 616 (9th Cir. 1965), "the findings made on motion for preliminary injunction, even though they relate, in whole or in part, to issues going to the merits of the case, are not determinative of those issues at trial." Because the interlocutory injunction, as well as the findings that support it, is merely provisional pending decision on the full hearing, the parties are not bound as by *res judicata*. The only carryover is that generally evidence offered at the interlocutory stage may be considered as evidence going to the merits of the case for purposes of the final decision.

j. EFFECT OF STATUTE ON THE DISCRETION OF THE COURT

In interpreting statutes dealing with the issuance of interlocutory injunctions, equity courts have jealously guarded the realm of their discretion. They have generally refused to allow apparent statutory mandates to reduce their function to that of a rubber stamp. For example, in

Mongogna v. O'Dwyer, 204 La. 1030, 16 So.2d 829 (1943), the petitioner sought a temporary restraining order enjoining gambling activity at the respondent's club. A state statute declared gambling houses to be nuisances, and provided that when a petition for an injunction was filed under the act, supported by the *ex parte* affidavits of two reputable citizens stating matters within their own knowledge and establishing the existence of the nuisance, the court "shall forthwith issue a temporary restraining order, to be in force until the hearing of the rule to show cause under Section 5 of this act; and said temporary restraining order shall prohibit the use of the place where said nuisance is averred to exist for any purpose, or purposes, whatsoever pending the trial and determination of the said rule to show cause." The court refused to interpret the statute as imposing a mandatory duty on the judge to issue a temporary restraining order in spite of the clear language of the statute. It stated, "We know of no case, and have been referred to none, upholding a statutory provision granting the absolute right to private parties to close a business by means of a restraining order issued through the instrumentality of the trial judge whose mandatory duty under the statute is to sign the order whether or not in his opinion it meets the exigencies of the case. The affirmance of such a proposition implies that the judge is nothing more than a rubber stamp whose only duty is to place his stamp of approval upon the demand of private parties, irrespective of whether or not he may consider that the demand is well founded. It necessarily divests the judge of his discretionary power to dispense with notice to the opposite party in one of the exceptional cases which may require the exercise of such power."

2. TYPES OF INTERLOCUTORY INJUNCTIONS

There are basically two types of interlocutory injunctions, distinguished from each other mainly by the procedure by which they are obtained. They are generally referred to as "preliminary injunctions" and "temporary restraining orders." All that has been said above in this chapter applies with equal force to each of these types of injunction. It would be well at this point to consider the features that distinguish the two types.

a. TEMPORARY RESTRAINING ORDERS

(i) *Generally*

The basic characteristic that sets temporary restraining orders apart from any other kind of injunction is that they can be issued *ex parte,* with no notice or opportunity to be heard afforded to the respondent. This apparent breach of the principles of due process is an accommodation to the emergency nature of cases in which the petitioner is under the threat of very serious irreparable injury of such immediacy that time does not permit observance of the usual requirements of notice and an opportunity to be heard. If, for example, a respondent is about to destroy or alter a piece of property which is the subject matter of litigation commenced by the petitioner, a temporary restraining order must be issued as soon as is practicably possible in order to hold the status quo, so that, as a practical matter, meaningful relief can be granted to the petitioner. If this practical circumstance does not allow time for the usual procedures of giving advance notice to the respondent and holding even an abbreviated hearing, it is well settled that it is not a denial of due process for the court to issue a temporary restraining order. In this way, the court can both grant emergency protection to the petitioner and preserve its own practical jurisdiction over the subject matter.

Needless to say, such an unusual power is closely ringed with limitations to prevent its abuse. For example, state statutes typically follow the requirements laid down by Rule 65 of the Federal Rules of Civil Procedure, which states:

> "A temporary restraining order may be granted without written or oral notice to the

adverse party or his attorney only if (1) it clearly appears from specific facts shown by affidavit or by the verified complaint that immediate and irreparable injury, loss, or damage will result to the applicant before the adverse party or his attorney can be heard in opposition, and (2) the applicant's attorney certifies to the court in writing the efforts, if any, which have been made to give the notice and the reasons supporting his claim that notice should not be required."

There is also generally a specific time limitation on the duration of temporary restraining orders fixed by statute. The most typical is the ten day limitation fixed by Rule 65. There is usually an added directive that the respondent is to be afforded an opportunity to be heard as soon as possible.

In addition to procedural limitations, there are also distinct discretionary limitations. A judge will generally be hesitant to issue an order in any but the most compelling circumstances when he can only guess at the potential effect on the respondent, and when he has not had the benefit of the most effective means of discovering both the law and the facts—adversary argument.

Although the temporary restraining order may be issued without notice, it is of no binding effect until notice of its existence reaches the respondent. This notice can come in many ways, from formal service by the appropriate officer, to communication by newspaper, telephone or telegraph. The two requirements are (1) that the means of communication chosen be entitled to *reasonable belief* by the respondent, and (2) that it convey specifically what the respondent is ordered to do or refrain from doing.

Just as with other interlocutory injunctions, a temporary restraining order follows the usual rules regarding mandatory and prohibitory orders. Preservation of the status quo is its proper function, whether by affirmative or negative order. For example, in Texas-Pipeline Co. v. Burton Drilling Co., 54 S.W.2d 190 (Tex.Civ.App. 1932), the respondent, a common carrier, refused to accept the oil of the petitioner into its delivery pipelines for the alleged purpose of deliberately damaging the petitioner's business and driving out small competitors of large oil companies. The petitioner had no storage facilities and no other means of delivery. It alleged that unless the respondent continued in the status quo of delivering petitioner's oil, it would evaporate, waste and depreciate in gasoline content. There the court issued an *ex parte* temporary restraining order, ordering the respondent to perform the *affirmative* act of delivering petitioner's oil in order to maintain the status quo of action.

[*184*]

In certain areas, the usual hesitancy of the court to issue an *ex parte* order has become practically an absolute refusal. The area of free speech is perhaps the most compelling. Any order which might place a prior restraint on free speech bears a heavy presumption of invalidity, and when the court is asked to restrain speech without affording the respondent a hearing on the matter, the presumption becomes practically impossible to overcome. In Carroll v. President and Commissioners of Princess Anne, 393 U.S. 175 (1968), a white racist group held a rally in the town, using insulting and threatening language. They invited the white members of the crowd back for a public rally the following night. The next day the town and county officials obtained an *ex parte* temporary restraining order without notice to the respondents, enjoining them from having rallies or meetings "which will tend to disturb and endanger the citizens of the County." On appeal, the Supreme Court declared the order invalid, stating, "There is a place in our jurisprudence for *ex parte* issuance, without notice, of temporary restraining orders of short duration; but there is no place within the area of basic freedoms guaranteed by the First Amendment for such orders where no showing is made that it is impossible to serve or to notify the opposing parties and to give them an opportunity to participate."

Notice the difference between *Carroll* and the case of Kingsley Books Inc. v. Brown, 354 U.S. 436 (1957), in which a preliminary injunction against the sale or distribution of obscene books was upheld. The major difference seemed to be that in *Kingsley Books* the respondent was given a hearing before issuance.

A second area in which the court's power to issue *ex parte* orders has been checked, this time by statute, is that of injunctions against strikes by labor unions. Congress recognized the seriousness of the harm caused by the numerous occurrences of "midnight injunctions," whereby an employer could disrupt the critical timing of a strike by obtaining an *ex parte* injunction on the eve of the strike. In that way, the union would be unable to take steps to obtain a hearing in time to preserve the timeliness of the strike. To restore the balance of power between labor and management, Congress passed the Norris-LaGuardia Act, Section 4 of which removed the power of federal courts of equity to enjoin most strikes.

(ii) Duty of the Respondent to Obey Temporary Restraining Order

Once a respondent receives notice of a temporary restraining order, his options are rather limited. Unless the court lacked personal jurisdiction over him, he is obliged to obey the order under penalty of at least criminal contempt, until he has obtained modification or nullification of the order by motion to the trial court or by appeal. Even if the court is ultimately found to have lacked jurisdiction over the subject matter of the action, under the rule of United States v. United Mine Workers, 330 U.S. 258 (1946), as long as the issue is arguable and not frivolous or feigned, the respondent would be subject to criminal contempt for violation of the order.

In the case of Walker v. City of Birmingham, 388 U.S. 307 (1967), the Supreme Court further defined the broad circumstances under which obedience to a temporary restraining order is required. The respondents were enjoined by a temporary restraining order, issued *ex parte*, from continuing their parades and demonstrations without obtaining a permit as required by the local ordinance. The respondents neither appealed nor moved to dissolve the injunction. Instead they called a press conference to state publically their intention to disregard the order and then proceeded to violate it. On appeal from their contempt citation, the respondents claimed that both the injunction and ordinance were unconstitutional. The Supreme Court affirmed the contempt conviction, stating that while the statute and injunction would both be subject to constitutional question because of vagueness and overbreadth, the respondents must raise the issue by a motion to dissolve or modify the injunction. The Court specified that, "An injunction duly issuing out of a court of general jurisdiction with equity powers, upon pleadings properly invoking its action, and served upon persons made parties therein and within the jurisdiction, must be obeyed by them, however erroneous the action of the court may be, even if the error be in the assumption of the validity of a seeming, but void law going to the merits of the case. It is for the court of first instance to determine the question of the validity of the law and until its decision is reversed for error by orderly review, either by itself or by a higher court, its orders based on its decision are to be respected, and disobedience of them is contempt of its lawful authority, to be punished." The Supreme Court was careful to note, however, that this rule is not so broad that it would permit the deliberate or systematic interference with a respondent's constitutional rights by procedural road blocks. In the Court's words, "This case would arise in quite a different constitutional posture if the petitioners, before disobeying the injunction, had challenged it in the Alabama courts, and had been met with delay or frustration of their constitutional claims."

The net result of the decisions discussed above is that while the law draws tight strings around the area of permissible *ex parte* injunctions, particularly in such areas as free speech or labor activities, it also severely restricts the procedure by which a respondent may challenge the permissibility of a particular injunction; and beyond those procedural limitations, the respondent's only option is to obey the injunction or be liable for contempt.

b.   PRELIMINARY INJUNCTIONS

There is little to add to the points already discussed in regard to interlocutory injunctions generally except to point out that a preliminary injunction differs from a temporary restraining order mainly in that it is issued only after a hearing is afforded to all parties concerned. It serves to preserve the status quo pending litigation in circumstances where relief, more immediate than the final decree on the merits is required, but not so immediate that it would defeat the purpose of the injunction to delay long enough to afford the respondent an opportunity to be heard. Because the respondent is able to present his side of the issue, the court is less leary of the possibility of visiting some serious unforeseen harm on him by issuing a preliminary injunction, than by issuing an *ex parte* temporary restraining order. Nevertheless, the court is aware of the truncated, frequently time-pressured nature of the hearing that is allowed to a respondent, as well as the incomplete state of the evidence on which it must act, and will therefore be more hesitant to affect seriously the life or business of the respondent by a preliminary injunction than by a final decree on the merits.   It is also true, however, that the limited duration of the preliminary injunction *may* lessen the seriousness of the imposition on the respondent, and this might serve to counterbalance the court's apprehension.

Other material features necessary to an understanding of the nature of the preliminary injunction are contained in the discussion of interlocutory injunctions generally.

C. PERMANENT INJUNCTIONS

Since this book deals mainly with the subject of permanent injunctions, most of the characteristics and incidents necessary to an understanding of the subject are discussed in other chapters. For the sake of clarifying the distinction between interlocutory and permanent injunctions, however, it might be valuable to discuss here the differences and similarities between the two.

1. SIMILARITIES

Among the characteristics that are common to all injunctions, permanent and interlocutory, the following are the most significant:

  a. The rules regarding jurisdiction and who can be bound by the court's order are uniform for all injunctions.

b. The methods of enforcement through civil and criminal contempt sanctions are generally the same.

c. As long as an injunction of either type is outstanding, the trial court retains jurisdiction (except when the case has been removed to the appellate court during the pendency of an appeal) to modify, vacate, or enforce the order on motion of the petitioner or respondent as circumstances evolve.

2. DIFFERENCES

a. The primary difference lies in the distinct purposes to be served by the two types of injunctions. Interlocutory injunctions are intended to serve the *sole* function of retaining the status quo between the parties to prevent irreparable harm and to preserve the court's ability to grant meaningful relief. The court is under no such restriction in granting a permanent injunction after full hearing and argument on the merits. The court is free to compel an alteration of circumstances between the parties to bring them into accord with the court's understanding of justice and equity. The court is also not limited to an affirmative or negative form of relief. It is only subject to the principles of equity discussed in Chapter III above.

b. There is no time limit imposed upon injunctive relief granted by way of a final decree. A permanent injunction will remain in force until it is modified or vacated by the trial or appellate court on request of the petitioner or respondent because of error in the decree or changed circumstances making the injunction inappropriate for the purpose of effecting equity and justice between the parties. An interlocutory injunction expires when the relatively short term of its function expires. For example, the life of a temporary restraining order is limited by statute, generally to a term of no longer than ten days. A preliminary injunction has served its total purpose when the court enters a final decree in the case, and at that point it is dissolved.

c. While the court balances the equities between petitioner and respondent in considering any injunction, it is more prone to give *equal* weight to the respective hardships of the respondent and petitioner in the case of an interlocutory injunction. Since at that early stage the petitioner has not yet established his right to relief on the merits, the parties stand equal before the court, and the court is as concerned over the harm its interlocutory injunction will do to the respondent as it is over the harm the petitioner will suffer without it. After a full hearing on the merits, wherein the petitioner has established the unlawfulness of the respondent's conduct and the injustice of the irreparable injury he will be caused by that conduct, the court does not *weigh* the harms equally. If the petitioner has established that he is otherwise entitled to injunctive relief, it will take more than equal, in fact quite serious, harm to the respondent to convince the court that equitable relief should not be granted (see the discussion of Balancing the Equities above in Chapter IV.)

d. Generally, by statute, the petitioner is required to post a bond in an amount specified by the court to indemnify the respondent against harm caused by an erroneously issued interlocutory injunction. This is in recognition of the fact that the court is, of necessity, acting under severe time pressures without adequate opportunity for evidence or argument. In this situation, the risk of an erroneous order is justified by the exigencies of the situation, and the bond minimizes the risk. Since a permanent injunction is only issued after both sides have had full opportunity to introduce evidence, cross-examine witnesses, and brief the law, the danger of an erroneous decree is reduced to a minimum. Therefore, it is a general rule that the petitioner is not required to post a bond as a condition to obtaining a permanent injunction.

e. Since the court is not required by the pressures of time to adopt procedural shortcuts in conducting a full hearing on the merits, the usual rules of evidence apply; and such things as affidavits and verified complaints, the usual bases for temporary restraining orders, are again subject to the rules of hearsay.

D. PROCEDURE

To see how each type of injunction fits into the procedural scheme, it might be well to trace the sequence of a typical situation. Assume that the respondent is threatening an unlawful invasion of the rights of the petitioner that will cause him irreparable injury. The petitioner is in need of a *permanent* injunction; and since the respondent threatens to violate his rights almost immediately, he will need immediate *temporary* relief as well. At this stage, the petitioner's counsel would prepare a bill in equity, stating the facts of the case and asking for appropriate relief. He would file the bill and have process served on the respondent in order to obtain personal jurisdiction. At the time of the filing of the bill he would present a petition to the court seeking issuance of an immediate temporary restraining order based upon the verified petition of his client and such affidavits as time would permit him to obtain, substantiating the factual basis for the petition. If the court were to grant the temporary restraining order, petitioner's counsel would file whatever bond was required by the court and see to it that notice of the temporary restraining order was issued to the respondent. The earliest possible time would be set by the court for a hearing by both parties on the issuance of a preliminary injunction. At that hearing, the issue basically would be whether or not the court should continue an order in force, this time termed a "preliminary injunction," restraining the respondent from altering the last uncontested status quo until the court could issue a final decree on the merits. If the preliminary injunction is issued, the respondent has three choices prior to the time of the hearing on the merits: (1) he can simply obey the injunction, (2) he can take an immediate appeal to a higher court, challenging the preliminary injunction as erroneous in form, scope, or basis, or (3) he can move the issuing court to vacate or modify the order on the basis of a change in circumstances occurring between the time of its issuance and the time of its dissolution when the final decree is entered.

The next step is the full hearing on the merits of the petition, followed by a final decree granting or denying a permanent injunction. The preliminary injunction is dissolved at that point. If the permanent injunction is granted, the respondent is then generally allowed a fixed number of days within which to appeal to a higher court. If he fails to appeal, he is precluded from attacking the permanent injunction further on the grounds that it is erroneous and his only alternative is to obey it or be subject to contempt proceedings. If, during the unlimited life of the permanent injunction, changed circumstances would justify its modification or dissolution, he may so move the issuing court. Otherwise the injunction will continue *ad infinitum*.

CHAPTER VI

EXTRATERRITORIAL EFFECT

A. RES JUDICATA

The conclusive effect to be given to injunctive decrees by courts of states other than that of the issuing court depends, to some extent, on the subject matter of the injunction. As a general guiding principle, the greater the element of *discretion* involved in selecting the particular form of injunction to be granted, the less conclusive effect it need be given under the full faith and credit clause of the Constitution. Discussion under the following categories will point up this principle.

1. MONEY DECREES

It is a general rule that an equitable decree that the respondent pay a fixed sum of money, currently due and owing, will be given the same full faith and credit as a money judgment issued by a court of law. As with a legal judgment, this does not mean that the equitable decree can simply be taken into another jurisdiction and directly executed by the sheriff of that jurisdiction. A separate action in a court of that second jurisdiction must be instituted so that a judgment or decree of that court may be obtained by the petitioner for execution by the sheriff. The sufficient basis for that second judgment, after personal jurisdiction over the respondent is obtained in the second jurisdiction, is the equitable decree of the first jurisdiction. Under the full faith and credit clause, the court of the second jurisdiction will consider the first equitable decree conclusive as to the rights of the parties and all factual issues that were decided by the first court. The respondent will not be allowed to challenge the validity of the decree of the first court during the action in the second jurisdiction on any ground other than fraud by the petitioner in obtaining it, or lack of personal or subject matter jurisdiction by the first court.

In this type of decree for the payment of a fixed sum of money currently due, there is practically no element of discretion. Once the facts establish that the respondent owes a certain sum to the petitioner, there is no basis for choice among alternative forms of decree by way of relief. A simple order that the respondent pay the sum to the petitioner is practically dictated. This type of decree will receive the complete conclusive effect as to both facts and rights of the parties detailed above.

2. DISCRETIONARY DECREES

At the other extreme, there are injunctive decrees that are drawn from a broad discretionary range of possibilities. For example, in the case of a nuisance action, once the equity court has established in its fact finding the existence, type, and seriousness of a nuisance, the court has a broad range of possible injunctions from which to draw in selecting relief appropriate to the equities between the parties. The possibilities run the gamut from no injunctive relief at all, leaving the petitioner to an action at law for damages; to an order that the respondent make appropriate changes in his operation to accommodate the rights of the petitioner; to an order that the respondent cease his operations altogether. In such a case, the choice of a particular form of decree depends solely on the discretion of the trial judge; and unlike an immutable finding of fact or order for the payment of money, the "final" order of the court in this instance is changeable at any time by that trial court if the circumstances of the parties should change. In such cases, courts of other jurisdictions will give the decree a very limited conclusive effect under the full faith and credit clause. If, for example, the respondent should remove himself and his property to another jurisdiction, so that the petitioner must seek similar relief there, that second jurisdiction will accept as conclusive all findings of fact litigated by the parties in the first proceeding, but will not give conclusive effect to the final injunctive order. The second jurisdiction will reserve the right to select its own form of injunctive relief based on those findings of fact.

This limited conclusive effect will apply in cases of nuisance, unfair competition, invasion of privacy, anti-trust violation, or any case wherein the final decree is selected from a broad range of possibilities as a matter of discretion.

3. DECREES ORDERING CONVEYANCES OF LAND INTERESTS

Between the two types of decrees discussed above, non-discretionary and broadly discretionary, lies the peculiar situation of decrees ordering conveyance of land interests. It must first be noted that an action to settle questions of ownership or possession of land is generally considered "local," as opposed to "transitory." This means that only the courts of the jurisdiction in which the land is located are considered to have subject matter jurisdiction over the action. The traditional exceptions are cases based on contract, trust, or fraud, and more recently, actions for property settlements in matrimonial disputes. In these cases, courts will enter decrees for conveyance of land lying outside of the boundaries of its jurisdiction. The conclusive effect to be given such decrees by courts of the jurisdiction in which the property is located is a matter of some disagreement.

The clearest rule, agreed to by all jurisdictions, is that all findings of fact which were, or could have been litigated at the will of the parties are given *res judicata* effect. A second unanimously accepted rule is that if any court orders the respondent to execute a deed conveying an interest in land, and under the threat of imposition of contempt sanctions the respondent obeys, the deed executed by the respondent himself will be accepted as valid by courts of the *situs* jurisdiction. This is true even where the decree ordering conveyance could not be obtained by the petitioner in the *situs* jurisdiction because of the local law or policy of that jurisdiction. If, for example, the court of jurisdiction A were to order the respondent to convey land located in jurisdiction B in satisfaction of a gambling debt, and the respondent did execute the required deed, the courts of the *situs* jurisdiction would recognize the deed as valid, even though gambling debts were unenforceable as contrary to public policy in the *situs* jurisdiction.

A third universally accepted rule is that if an equity court orders that its decree shall, in and of itself, be effective to transfer the title to foreign property as under a vesting statute, or appoints a master or commissioner to execute the conveyance of foreign property as under an appointive statute (see the discussion of vesting and appointive statutes above in Chapter II), no effect whatever will be given to such attempted conveyance.

The major point of disagreement is the effect to be given to the portion of a decree which determines "the equities between the parties"—that is, the determination that the petitioner is entitled to have the respondent convey a property interest to him in cases in which the respondent has failed to honor the decree by personally executing the deed. Stated another way, courts disagree as to whether or not conclusive effect is to be given to a decree of a non-*situs* court, declaring the equitable interest of a petitioner in land.

Some courts group this type of case with those involving discretionary decrees and consider as conclusive only findings of fact, such as the execution and validity of a contract for the sale of land. The basis for the court's assumed power to refuse conclusive effect to the determination of rights and equities of the parties is the theory that such determinations are beyond the scope of the full faith and credit clause. This makes it a matter of comity as to whether or not the court will give conclusive effect to the ultimate decree of its sister court. The three most common reasons for refusing to grant comity to such ultimate decrees are the following:

a. A DIFFERENCE IN POLICIES BETWEEN THE SITUS JURISDICTION AND THE JURISDICTION OF THE COURT ISSUING THE DECREE, SUCH THAT THE DECREE WOULD BE UNOBTAINABLE IN THE SITUS JURISDICTION

It seems somewhat anomalous that a *situs* jurisdiction would recognize as unassailable a deed executed by a respondent under the duress of a foreign decree that would not be granted for policy reasons in the *situs* jurisdiction, and yet that it would insist on its freedom to refuse to recognize the decree itself if the respondent had been swift enough to escape enforcement of the decree by the issuing court. Nevertheless, some states have adopted this gerrymandered view of the full faith and credit clause.

b. DISAPPROVAL OF AN ERROR OF LAW ON THE PART OF THE ISSUING COURT

If the full faith and credit clause were found applicable, the *situs* court would not have the luxury of choosing not to recognize the decree, regardless of how erroneous it might be, as long as it was not obtained by fraud and there was no defect in jurisdiction. Once the obstacle of full faith and credit is obviated by close interpretation, the *situs* court is free to allow collateral attack of the decree by simply refusing to accept it as a matter of comity.

c.   EFFECT ON THE RECORDING SYSTEM

Although some courts have cited the possible disruption of the local recording system as a reason for denying full recognition to the foreign decree, this seems an illusory hurdle. To create a recordable interest, the petitioner would only have to sue on the foreign decree and obtain a decree of the *situs* court. Short of this, any bona fide transferee of an interest in the land without actual notice of the equitable interest would take free and clear of that interest. Whatever interest was decreed by the foreign court would cause no greater disruption than any other unrecorded equitable interest. Any added uncertainty that this might cause would seem to be counterbalanced by the advantages of 1) a more reasonable, consistent application of the full faith and credit clause, and 2) an elimination of the need for double trial of the same issue.

The second view, which is coming to be accepted in an increasing number of jurisdictions, is that expressed by the Ohio court in Burnley v. Stevenson, 24 Ohio St. 474 (1873):

"The constitution of the United States declares that full faith and credit shall be given in each state to the records and judicial proceedings of every other state, and provides that Congress may prescribe the mode of proving such records and proceedings, and the effect thereof. By an act of May 26, 1790, Congress declared that the 'records and judicial proceedings of the state courts,' when properly authenticated, 'shall have the same faith and credit given to them in every court within the United States, as they have, by law or usage, in the courts of the state from whence they are or shall be taken.' When, therefore, a decree rendered by a court in a sister state, having jurisdiction of the parties and of the subject-matter, is offered as evidence, or pleaded as the foundation of a right, in any action in the courts of this state, it is entitled to the same force and effect which it had in the state where it was pronounced. . . . True, the courts of this state can not enforce the performance of that decree, by compelling the conveyance through its process of attachment; but when pleaded in our courts as a cause of action, or as a ground of defense, it must be regarded as conclusive of all the rights and equities which were adjudicated and settled therein, unless it be impeached for fraud."

In jurisdictions of this type, cases may arise in which the decree of a foreign court is in such serious conflict with the public policy of the state in which it is sought to be enforced that important interests of the state would be jeopardized by blind application of the full faith and credit clause. This is perhaps the greatest fear of those jurisdictions that hold that the full faith and credit clause does not apply to foreign decrees as to the equities between the parties. There is, however, in constitutional theory, a solution to this problem. If the conflict is so severe that serious state interests are affected, an exception to the full faith and credit clause is implied. The test applied by the Supreme Court is basically a determination in each case of whether or not the harm done by applying the full faith and credit clause overshadows the general benefit to be derived from its application. Such cases are extremely infrequent. As a general rule only the interests of isolated individuals will be affected with no serious disruption to general state policies.

B. COMITY

Beyond the area controlled by the full faith and credit clause is a broad area in which a court *may* recognize and follow a sister court's decree as a matter of comity. This area will be considered from two points of view: (1) that of the court which is being asked to grant comity, and (2) that of the court about to issue a decree that will depend for its effectiveness upon the comity of a sister court.

1. CONSIDERATIONS OF A COURT ASKED TO GRANT COMITY

As a general rule a court will be disposed to grant comity by way of accepting a sister court's decree unless there is some serious reason for refusing it. The reasons for this inclination are (a) the general interest in fostering friendly relations between neighboring states, and (b) the desire for reciprocal treatment of its own decrees. This will lead a court to overlook conflicts in policy that have no serious effect on the state's interest when it has no cause to believe that its citizens are being dealt with unjustly. In the case of McElreath v. McElreath, 162 Tex. 190, 345 S.W. 2d 722 (1961), for example, a husband and wife, domiciled in Oklahoma, were divorced in Oklahoma. The decree of the Oklahoma court ordered the husband to convey land in Texas to the wife as part of the alimony settlement. The husband skipped across the border to Texas before the decree could be enforced. The wife sued on the decree in the Texas court. The policy of Texas in regard to alimony was practically the opposite of that of Oklahoma. In Texas, no permanent alimony could be granted, nor could a Texas court divest either spouse of his or her separate property. A wife must simply look to her share of community property. Nevertheless, the Texas court recognized and followed the Oklahoma decree as a matter of comity. The reasons were well stated as follows:

> "As a matter of justice, good order and common sense, the Oklahoma decree should be enforced in Texas, unless contrary to some well defined public policy of this State. There is something incongruous and out of keeping with the concept of orderly processes to tolerate a situation wherein solemn court decrees may be flouted by playing hop-skip with state boundaries. This case involves Oklahomans and it is not against the public policy of Texas for Oklahoma to maintain a different system of property ownership for its residents than that provided by Texas for Texans. . . . We expect other states to recognize our system of marital property ownership, so should

[*208*]

we respect their schemes of property ownership and attendant plans for the adjustment
of property rights upon the dissolution of a
marriage."

At times, the conflicting policies of the state
can outweigh considerations favoring comity.
For example, in DeBrimont v. Penniman, Fed.
Cas.No.3,715, 10 Blatchf. 436 (1873), the respondent's daughter married a citizen of France
and became domiciled there with him. The respondent, an American, visited his daughter and
son-in-law in France and was there served with
process in a suit by the son-in-law under a
French statute which provided that a father-in-
law is legally obliged to provide for the support
of his son-in-law, regardless of the lack of effort
by the son-in-law to support himself. The
French Court entered a decree for the son-in-law,
ordering the respondent to make monthly payments. The respondent returned to America
without honoring the decree. The son-in-law
came to America and filed a bill against the respondent based on the French decree. The
American Court refused to consider the decree
binding on the respondent. The court held (a)
that the full faith and credit clause does not require that conclusive effect be given to the
French decree because that clause is limited to
relationships between the states, and (b) that
comity would not be extended to the French de-

cree because (1) it was not based on principles of universal acceptation, such as the obligation of contracts or the protection of generally recognized personal rights or obligations such as the support of *minor* children; and (2) it was, in fact, potentially contrary to American policy to compel the support of a son-in-law in idleness while he is under no obligation to support himself.

2. CONSIDERATIONS OF A COURT ISSUING A DECREE WHICH WILL REQUIRE COMITY OF A SISTER COURT FOR EFFECTIVENESS

In deciding whether or not a sister court will grant comity to its decree if issued, a court will view the same considerations discussed above from the point of view of the other court.   For example, in Hertz System Inc. v. McIllree, 26 Ill. App.2d 390, 168 N.E.2d 468 (1960), a United States citizen brought a bill in equity in Illinois against a citizen of Australia for an order that the respondent specifically perform a contract to transfer Australian trademark registrations. The respondent was personally served with process in Illinois, but soon departed for Australia. It was obvious that any decree issued by the Illinois court would only be effective if it could be sued upon in Australia. The order was issued by the trial court and affirmed on appeal. After carefully reviewing Australian law and policy on the transfer of trademark registrations, the appellate court stated, "In our opinion the decree does not encroach on the sovereign power of Australia nor offend fundamental policy of British courts against the enforcement of foreign judgments violating fundamental notions of justice."

On this basis, the court had sufficient reason to believe that its order would not be rendered useless by a denial of comity and should therefore be issued.

One further case might be useful to illustrate the thinking process of a court on this point. In United States v. Ross, 196 F.Supp. 243 (S.D.N.Y. 1961), an action was brought under the Internal Revenue Code seeking appointment of a receiver for respondent's property and an order that the respondent endorse and deliver to the receiver stock certificates of a corporation incorporated in the Bahamas, all in aid of collecting overdue taxes. There was no doubt of the court's power to order the transfer, but a serious question was raised as to whether or not the courts of the Bahamas would recognize the transfer because of the principle that one state or nation will not enforce the tax laws of another state or nation. The court decided to issue the order, stating, "I doubt whether this principle would be pushed so far that, if defendant, under compulsion of an order of this court, transferred title to the shares to a receiver appointed by this court and the receiver sold them in order to raise money to pay the taxes, the court in the Bahamas would refuse to recognize the title of the purchaser. I further doubt that the courts of the Bahamas would refuse to recognize directors elected by the receiver as a stockholder."

An example of the reasoning of a state court in considering the possibilities of comity from courts of sister states occurred in Madden v. Rosseter, 114 Misc. 416, 187 N.Y.S. 462 (1921). Petitioner and respondent contracted to share the services of a race horse, the respondent to race him in California for two years, and the petitioner to race him in Kentucky for the next two years. When the time came, the respondent refused to send the horse to Kentucky, and the petitioner brought a bill in equity against him in New York where personal service could be obtained. The petitioner asked that a receiver be appointed to go to California and invoke the aid of the courts there to recover possession of the horse. The obvious drawback was that a commissioner appointed by the New York court would have no power beyond the New York state line. Nevertheless, the court granted the order, stating, "The courts of sister states may be relied upon to aid in serving the ends of justice when-

ever our own process falls short of effectiveness."
One convincing feature, typical of this type of
case, was that no other jurisdiction could give
more complete relief, since the power of each
would be limited to its geographical boundaries.

C. JURISDICTION OF AN EQUITY COURT TO AFFECT OUT OF STATE PROPERTY OR ACTIVITY

It has been conceded since the early days of equity jurisdiction, that as long as a court had personal jurisdiction of the respondent, it was well
within its power to order him to perform acts
within the jurisdiction, even though the property
to be affected lay outside of the jurisdiction.
This is particularly true of such cases as nuisance
actions, or actions concerning the use or diversion of waterways, since in many instances the
forum state is the only state in which personal
jurisdiction of the respondent can be obtained.

In actions involving the transfer of title to
property, however, only those based on contract,
trust, fraud, or marital rights, are considered
"transitory" so that suit can be brought in other
than the *situs* jurisdiction. All other forms of
such action are considered "local" so that only
the *situs* court has subject matter jurisdiction.

[*213*]

In the reverse situation, that is, a bill in equity for an order that the respondent do or refrain from doing something outside of the jurisdiction that will affect property lying within the jurisdiction, the courts are agreed that there is subject matter jurisdiction. The most famous case of this type was The Salton Sea Cases, 172 F. 792 (9th Cir., 1909), wherein the petitioner's land in California was subject to flooding caused by the respondent's diverting of water from the Colorado River. To correct the situation, the respondent would have to construct restraints in Mexico. The court found no lack of power or appropriateness in issuing the order.

The major drawback in this latter type of case is not jurisdictional. It is the problem of convincing the court that it will meet no insurmountable obstacles in supervising and enforcing adequate performance of its order, and that its order will not conflict with the building codes or other laws or policies of the state where performance is to take place. The court in *The Salton Sea* Cases neatly dodged the problem by simply negatively restraining the respondent from allowing the flooding to occur in California because of its diversion of the waterway. The fact that this would, of necessity, require the respondent to construct water restraints in Mexico was the respondent's problem. The court was *indirectly* ordering the respondent to build the restraints without embroiling itself in concern over possible conflict with Mexican law or policy, or the difficulties of extra-territorial supervision.

The third possible situation is that in which out-of-state performance is to be required which will affect or protect out-of-state property. The Supreme Court, in Northern Indiana R. Co. v. Michigan Cent. R. Co., 56 U.S. 233 (1853), definitively declared that such an action must be brought in the jurisdiction where performance of the court's order is to occur or where the property to be affected is located. All other courts lack subject matter jurisdiction. (See affirmation of this rule in *The Salton Sea* Cases, supra.)

CHAPTER VII

ENFORCEMENT OF INJUNC-
TIONS—CONTEMPT

A. GENERAL

With the exception of specialized procedures for the enforcement of decrees in limited types of situations, such as conveyance of title under a vesting or appointive statute, the only practical force available to the court for enforcement of its decrees is its ability to impose contempt sanctions on the respondent. In a practical sense, the concept of contempt power goes hand in hand with that of jurisdiction. In the beginning of this book, personal jurisdiction was defined in terms of the ability of the court to impose contempt sanctions on the respondent for disobedience of its order without violating his constitutional right of due process. As a practical matter, without contempt power to put teeth in the court's order, jurisdictional power would be an empty illusion.

An efficient, orderly, procedural scheme has evolved whereby an equity court can make skillful use of the only two sanctions available to it, imprisonment and fine, to apply the right amount of pressure to the respondent to accomplish the specific result desired at any point in the litigation.   Unfortunately, most instances of inefficient or erroneous application of this delicate power result from a lack of understanding of the procedural scheme.   This is unfortunate, because in the hands of an informed and temperate judge, contempt procedure can function like a scalpel in the hands of a skilled surgeon.

B.   TYPES OF CONTEMPT

There are two distinct types of contempt, *criminal* and *civil*, which differ from each other in both function and procedure.   Ninety percent of the malfunctions in the system of contempt result from confusion of the distinctions between these two types of contempt; but once mastered, the rules governing their application follow a consistent, logical pattern.

1.   CRIMINAL CONTEMPT

As the name implies, criminal contempt is punitive in nature.   It is intended to serve the interests of the *court* and *society generally* by punishing a respondent for deliberate violation of the court's order, and by deterring future violation in much the same way that other criminal penalties are intended to deter violations of the criminal law.   The term generally used to describe this function is "vindication of the authority of the court." The petitioner is benefited by criminal contempt only in the incidental way that a particular victim of a crime is benefited when the perpetrator of the crime is subjected to criminal penalties.

To warrant criminal contempt sanctions, the act of the respondent need not be a violation of any law other than the order of the court. A number of courts hold that it is sufficient if (a) the respondent deliberately performs an act or refusal to act, and (b) that act or refusal to act violates an order of the court. (Some of these jurisdictions will not even accept as a defense the respondent's good faith reliance on advice of counsel that his act will not violate the court's order.) Other courts require both that the respondent act or refuse to act deliberately and that he *be aware* at the time of his act or refusal that he is violating the court's order.

The fact that a violation has occurred may be brought to the court's attention by the petitioner, possibly by way of a petition for civil contempt; but the criminal contempt process is considered an action separate and distinct from the original action in which the injunction was issued. It is prosecuted, not by the petitioner, but by the judge himself, or an officer of the court. As is frequently done, however, it is possible to combine a hearing on criminal contempt with a hearing on civil contempt, as long as the more rigorous procedural requirements for criminal contempt are observed. Since the criminal contempt process is considered a separate action, it can be prosecuted even though the original injunctive action is dismissed or lost by the petitioner on the merits, as long as an injunction of the court was in force at the time of the violation.

In considering the amount of the fine or prison sentence to be imposed for criminal contempt, the court will consider the following criteria:

(a) The extent of culpability or willfulness of defiance of the court's order;

(b) The seriousness of the consequences to the petitioner and the public generally of the respondent's disobedience;

(c) The necessity for deterring future violations by the respondent;

(d) The need to set an example to deter violations by others and promote respect for court orders generally;

(e) The effect on the respondent of any particular sentence or fine (a $1,000 fine may be devastating to one respondent but no more than a slap on the wrist to another).

Since the courts have recognized the similarities between criminal contempt and other forms of criminal actions in their effect on the respondent, it has become an accepted principle that the constitutional safeguards that protect a defendent in a criminal trial also apply to criminal contempt proceedings. As early as 1911, the Supreme Court held in Gompers v. Bucks Stove and Range Co., 221 U.S. 418 (1911), that the respondent in a criminal contempt proceeding is presumed innocent until proven guilty beyond a reasonable doubt, and that he cannot be compelled to testify against himself.

In 1925, in Cooke v. United States, 267 U.S. 517 (1925), the Court held that a respondent in criminal contempt has a right to "assistance of counsel, if requested, and the right to call witnesses to give testimony, relevant either to the issue of complete exculpation or in extenuation of the offense and in mitigation of the penalty to be imposed."

In 1948, the Court decided the case of In re Oliver, 333 U.S. 257 (1948). There a single justice, doubling as a one-man grand jury and trial judge under Michigan procedure, disbelieved a witness' testimony before him as grand juror and sentenced him to sixty days in prison for criminal contempt as trial judge, all in secret session. In reviewing the proceeding, the Supreme Court held that the right to a public trial applied to all criminal contempt proceedings.

In 1968, an important ruling was made in Bloom v. Illinois, 391 U.S. 194 (1968). Previously, criminal contempt had been classified as a "petty offense" to which the constitutional right to a jury trial did not attach. In *Bloom*, the court held that the distinction between a "petty" and a "serious" offense should depend on the seriousness of the penalty imposed, and that when the penalty exceeds some unspecified degree of seriousness, the respondent has the right to a jury trial. The court reasoned that the buffer of jury trial is even more essential to a criminal contempt proceeding than to the average criminal trial because often the respondent's violation of the court's own order strikes at the most vulnerable and human qualities of the judge's temperament. In Dyke v. Taylor Implement Co., 391 U.S. 216 (1968), the Court rounded out the *Bloom Rule* by adopting the federal statutory definition of a "petty" offense as one for which the penalty does not exceed imprisonment for more than six months or a fine of $500, or both. (See 18 U.S. C.A. § 1). In Frank v. United States, 395 U.S. 147 (1969), the Court added a new dimension by holding that the penalty of probation for up to five years would be within the "petty" category.

In the Dyke v. Taylor Implement Co. case cited above, the Court also held that evidence seized in violation of the Fourth or Fourteenth Amendment would be subject to the exclusionary rule of

Mapp v. Ohio, 367 U.S. 643 (1961), in criminal contempt proceedings.

An important rule was also formulated in Argersinger v. Hamlin, 407 U.S. 25 (1972), for criminal trials in general. The court held that absent a knowing and intelligent waiver, no person may be imprisoned for any offense, whether classified as petty, misdemeanor, or felony, unless he was represented by counsel at his trial. It seems inevitable that this rule will be applied to criminal contempt proceedings, so that if *any* prison sentence is to be imposed as a criminal contempt sanction, the respondent must be afforded the right to counsel.

For the time being, therefore, the dividing line between a "petty" and a "serious" penalty differs depending upon which constitutional right is concerned. For instance, the respondent need not be afforded a jury trial unless the penalty actually imposed exceeds six months in prison or a $500 fine, or both. He must be afforded a right to counsel if a fine in excess of $500 or *any* term of imprisonment, or both, is imposed. He has the right to a public trial, notice of the charges, confrontation of witnesses, and the presumption of innocence if any penalty at all is imposed.

One major distinction between criminal contempt proceedings and other forms of criminal action is that in nearly half of the jurisdictions there is no fixed maximum penalty for criminal contempt. The general rule in criminal law is that a crime is considered "serious" or "petty," for purposes of constitutional rights, depending upon whether or not the maximum sentence fixed by statute exceeds the appropriate limit. This is known in advance of trial, and the trial procedure can, therefore, be accommodated to the constitutional requirements. In criminal contempt, however, since there is often no stated maximum sentence, the characterization of "serious" or "petty" depends upon the sentence actually imposed, which cannot be known prior to the termination of the proceeding. This leads to two results: (a) either a court will take the precaution of affording the respondent his maximum constitutional protections so that a serious penalty can be imposed if appropriate; or (b) the court will be forced to limit itself to penalties within the "petty" range to avoid reversal on constitutional grounds.

2. CIVIL CONTEMPT

The sole purpose of civil contempt is to serve the interests of the petitioner for whom the original injunction was issued. Only *he* has standing to petition the court for civil contempt for its violation. Unlike criminal contempt, a civil contempt proceeding is considered a mere continuation of the original action in which the injunction was issued, which means, among other things, that there is no need to acquire new personal jurisdiction over the respondent. Also, as with criminal contempt, only the court that issued the injunction has jurisdiction to enforce it by contempt proceedings.

There are two distinct types of civil contempt, each designed to serve a separate need of the petitioner.

a.   CIVIL CONTEMPT TO COMPEL COMPLIANCE

Once an injunction is issued and violated, the primary interest of the petitioner may be simply to obtain obedience to the injunction in the future. This may be accomplished by the civil contempt sanction of a *conditional* fine or imprisonment. For example, if a labor union is in violation of a court order enjoining a strike, the court might impose, by way of civil contempt, a conditional fine of $500 a day for every day in the future that the union continues its violation. Another example would be that of a respondent ordered to pay a certain amount each month in child support. If he were to refuse, he could be sentenced by way of civil contempt to a conditional term in prison—that is, he would remain in prison only until he agreed to obey the injunction. In this case, he is said to have the keys to the jail in his pocket. It is this ability to free himself by simply doing that which the court has determined that he ought to do in the first place that justifies imprisonment by civil process without the constitutional trappings that accompany a criminal contempt proceeding.

In fixing the amount of a conditional fine, the court will consider (a) the resources of the respondent for the purpose of judging the effectiveness of a fine in any particular amount toward inducing compliance by this respondent, and (b) the relative necessity of compliance to the petitioner (and the public).

Civil contempt to compel compliance is limited by two principles. The first was exemplified by the case of Application of McCausland, 130 Cal. App. 708, 279 P.2d 820 (1955). The respondent had failed to obey an order of the court to pay a sum of money to the petitioner. In a civil contempt proceeding, the court ordered him imprisoned until he should comply. The order of conditional imprisonment was reversed on appeal on the ground that there had been no finding that the respondent was *able* to obey the injunction. By way of comparison, in Reeves v. Crownshield, 274 N.Y. 74, 8 N.E.2d 283 (1937), the petitioner was granted a judgment for $400. When the judgment remained unsatisfied, the petitioner ob-

[225]

tained an order of the court that the respondent pay $20 a month until the judgment should be completely satisfied, commitment to prison to result if the respondent should fail. The monthly sum was fixed by the court after a consideration of the respondent's needs and his ability to pay. The respondent failed to meet the payments, and his imprisonment was upheld since the court had considered the question of his ability to pay at the time the payment order was issued.

The second principle affecting conditional imprisonment is that embodied in a number of state constitutions forbidding imprisonment for debt. This principle is more limited in its application than is generally believed because it is held to apply only to cases of debt arising from contracts. It does not apply to cases of fraud, trust, alimony or child support, willful injury to persons or property, or fines or penalties imposed by law.

b. CIVIL CONTEMPT TO COMPENSATE PETITIONER

The second type of civil contempt serves the function of financial compensation to the petitioner for damage caused by the violation of the court's order. This is accomplished by way of a fine payable to the petitioner. The amount of the fine is measured directly by the amount of damage suffered by the petitioner as a result of the violation.

In order to be entitled to this type of compensation the petitioner must win the case on the merits. This means that in the case of violation of an <u>interlocutory injunction</u>, the petitioner can obtain civil contempt to compel compliance as soon as a violation occurs, but <u>he cannot obtain civil contempt to compensate him for his damages until he wins the action on the merits</u>. In the event that it is a permanent injunction that is violated, the plaintiff will have already won the action on the merits, and can therefore be awarded compensation immediately. It should, however, be remembered that the awarding of all forms of civil contempt is discretionary with the court.

One situation that has caused some confusion is the following. In the event that a conditional fine is imposed in a civil contempt proceeding, and the respondent subsequently continues to violate the injunction, the court, after a hearing, can make the fine absolute. There is, however, some question as to whether that absolute fine is a civil or criminal contempt sanction. If the amount of the conditional fine was fixed with regard to the severity necessary to draw compliance out of the respondent, as is the usual case, then the same fine, when made absolute, must be paid to the court and not to the petitioner, since the petitioner can only be awarded the amount of his damages.   Therefore, although the conditional fine was imposed in a civil contempt proceeding, the absolute fine bears the marks of a criminal contempt sanction, and the proceeding in which it is imposed should measure up to the constitutional standards for criminal process.

C. DISTINGUISHING CIVIL FROM CRIMINAL CONTEMPT

Misunderstanding of the distinctions between civil and criminal contempt on the part of lawyers and judges has been responsible for many erroneous orders.   Much of the confusion can be eliminated by starting with the proposition that the distinctive features of civil or criminal contempt do not inhere in the act of violation itself.   The same act can frequently result in either civil or criminal contempt sanctions or both.   It has even been held that it does not violate the double jeopardy provision of the Constitution to impose both kinds of contempt sanctions for the same act.   What actually categorizes the violation of the court's order as criminal or civil contempt is the adjudication of the court, after a hearing, in which one or the other form of penalty is imposed.   It is much like the three umpires who were discussing their methods of calling balls and strikes. The first said he "calls 'em as he sees 'em." The second said he "calls 'em as they are." The third disagreed with both and said "Until I calls 'em, they ain't nothin!" And so it is with violations of injunctions. Until the judge calls them civil or criminal by imposing the appropriate sanction, they do not inherently bear the character of either.

The consequences of the distinction between civil and criminal contempt are numerous and important. Some of the most critical are the following.

1. CONSTITUTIONAL PROCEDURES

As discussed above, in order to validly support the imposition of criminal contempt sanctions, the respondent must be given a hearing in which the required constitutional protections are afforded. Since these protections are not necessary in a hearing for civil contempt, it is important for the court to foresee before the hearing begins whether it will wish to impose criminal sanctions or merely civil sanctions, and then to shape the proceeding accordingly. Often a court can make this prediction accurately on the basis of its prior knowledge of the case, the parties, their attitudes, and the type and seriousness of the alleged violation.

2. APPLICATION OF CRIMINAL STATUTE OF LIMITATIONS

Although a criminal statute of limitations may bar the imposition of criminal contempt sanctions under local interpretation, it would have no effect on civil contempt sanctions.

3. CONSEQUENCES OF PETITIONER'S VOLUNTARY DISMISSAL OF THE ACTION

If the petitioner should at any time voluntarily dismiss his injunctive action, he would lose the ability to obtain civil contempt sanctions, either to compel performance or to compensate him for damages from violation of any previous order. Dismissal would not, however, deprive the court of the power to impose criminal contempt sanctions for violation of any order outstanding during the pendency of the action.

4. PROCEDURE AND SCOPE OF APPELLATE REVIEW

While an appellate court would review a criminal contempt proceeding with the same acceptance of the jury verdict as to facts and the same scrutiny as to procedure and the law as in the case of a criminal trial, it will review a civil contempt proceeding under the much different standards applied to any civil proceeding, tried by a judge without jury, resulting in a discretionary order. (See discussion of Appeal in Chapter VIII)

5. POWER OF THE EXECUTIVE TO PARDON

While the executive, in the person of a governor or the President, has the power to pardon one convicted of criminal contempt, the separation of powers principle precludes his pardoning a respondent who is subjected to civil contempt sanctions.

6. COSTS TO THE PETITIONER

While courts usually award costs to a petitioner who has successfully prosecuted a petition to hold the respondent in civil contempt, as a general rule costs are not added to criminal contempt sanctions. If, in an unusual criminal contempt proceeding, costs were assessed, they would be made payable to the government.

7. UNITED MINE WORKERS SITUATION

The Court in United States v. United Mine Workers, 330 U.S. 258 (1947), created the following small but important exception. Criminal contempt may be imposed for violation of an interlocutory injunction, issued to hold the status quo until the court can decide an arguable question of whether or not it has subject matter jurisdiction, even if it ultimately decides that it does not. Civil contempt will not lie if the petitioner loses on the issue of subject matter jurisdiction.

CHAPTER VIII

APPEAL

A. GENERAL

Appellate review of decisions of courts of equity differs from review of legal judgments in ways that reflect the basic differences between law and equity. The standard method of review at law is by *writ of error*. The basic question presented is whether or not the judgment should be reversed because of specific errors of law committed by the trial judge to which the appealing party took exception at the time. The appellate court does not concern itself with the fairness or justice of the judgment, nor with the resolution of questions of fact which must be left to the jury. It is only allowed to inquire into challenged rulings of law, such as rulings on admissability of evidence, or charges on the law to the jury.

An equity decree, on the other hand, is usually reviewed by an *appeal*; and the basic question is whether the decree issued is appropriate in the light of the entire case as disclosed by the record. In other words, the appellate court examines the result rather than specific legal steps taken in reaching it.

Two major points in common between review of equity and legal decisions are 1) that the time and procedure for review are governed in both cases exclusively by statute; and 2) that only parties adversely affected by the lower court's decision have standing to appeal it. This latter point is one of some importance to individuals who stand a good chance of being held in contempt for violation of a decree as aiders or abettors. Since they are not *parties* to the action in which the decree was entered, they have no standing to appeal it. To acquire standing, they could petition to intervene as parties in the action; and if there is sufficient danger of their being held in contempt as aiders or abettors, such a petition should generally be granted. The decision to intervene, however, raises the tactical question of whether or not the individual wishes to submit to personal jurisdiction at this time. That can frequently be a dilemma calling for careful, practical weighing of alternatives:—is the individual's status as an aider or abettor questionable, so that by remaining beyond the grasp of personal jurisdiction he might escape coverage by the decree altogether; or is his status fairly certain to be considered that of an aider or abettor so that he could only gain by intervening for purposes of appealing an erroneous decree. These decisions are seldom clear cut and often placed severe demands on the experience and psychic abilities of counsel.

B. APPEAL OF INJUNCTIONS

For purposes of analyzing the appellate procedure, a trial court's decision to grant or deny an injunction can be divided into three elements: 1) findings of fact, 2) rulings of law and 3) discretionary decisions in regard to fairness and justice between the petitioner, the respondent, and the public. The standards for reviewing each of these elements are distinct.

1. FINDINGS OF FACT

In reviewing a judgment at law, the appellate court is bound to accept findings of fact by the jury as conclusive in accordance with constitutional provisions for trial by jury. The situation is quite different in reviewing equitable decrees. Originally, all equitable matters were tried before the chancery on exclusively written evidence. Since the appellate court felt that it could read and interpret documentary evidence as well as the trial judge, the rule developed that all findings of fact were open to review *de novo*, as if no original findings had been made. This rule changed somewhat when the chancery court opened its proceedings to oral testimony from live witnesses. At that point, the trial judge had the important advantage of being able to observe the bearing, voice, and attitude of the witness testifying before him, and he was therefore in a better position than the appellate court to assess the truthfulness of the testimony. The rule for review became, therefore, that all findings of fact based on documentary or physical evidence *alone* would still be open to complete review *de novo*; but that findings of fact based on oral testimony of witnesses would not be reversed unless they were *clearly against the evidence*. Old Corner Book Store v. Upham, 194 Mass. 101, 80 N.E. 228 (1907). That is the rule today.

Because findings of fact in equity cases lack the conclusiveness of findings of fact in legal actions for purposes of appeal, and because the findings are usually made by experienced judges rather than laymen jurors, the usual rules of evidence that dictate what evidence should come to the attention of jurors play a far less significant role in equity actions. The appellate court in Shedd v. Seefeld, 230 Ill. 118, 82 N.E. 580 (1907), answered the point that errors were committed by the trial court in the admission and exclusion of evidence by saying, "This being a chancery proceeding, any error in this regard is unimportant if there is competent evidence in the record sufficient to support the decree, and the evidence which ought to have been considered would not, if considered, change the result."

2. RULINGS OF LAW

The standard for review of rulings of law in equity cases is practically the same as that in legal actions. The appellate court is free to interpret the law and apply it to the facts, unhindered by any ruling of law by the lower court. For example, in Douglas v. Beneficial Finance Co. of Anchorage, 469 F.2d 453 (9th Cir. 1972), the petitioner brought an equity action against the respondent loan companies for violations of the Federal Truth-in-Lending Act in failing to disclose as security interests certain confession of judgment clauses in their promissory notes. The trial court ruled that the clauses were security interests within the meaning of the Act and issued a preliminary injunction restraining the respondents from collecting on the notes pending the outcome of the action. The appellate court reversed the order, granting the injunction on the ground that under its interpretation of the Act, these confession of judgment clauses did not qualify as security interests. The court stated that "Ordinarily, the grant or denial of a preliminary injunction is a matter within the discretion of the district court, and it will not be reversed absent an abuse of that discretion. . . . An exception to this rule applies when such grant or denial is based upon an erroneous legal premise; the order is then reviewable as is any other conclusion of law."

In addition to the usual areas considered to be "rulings of law," such as interpretations of statutes and common law rules, appellate courts have held that the application of the equity principles that define equitable jurisdiction, such as the principle regarding adequacy of remedy at law, are also within this category. (See discussion of these principles in Chapter III above.) An appellate court is free to examine *de novo*, for example, whether on the evidence in the record the petitioner has an adequate remedy elsewhere. One exception to this rule is that if the respondent fails to raise an issue of lack of equity jurisdiction in the trial court, he will generally be held to have waived it, and will be precluded in most jurisdictions from raising it on appeal.

3. DISCRETION

The third crucial element of a decision to issue or withhold any injunction is the discretion of the trial judge in determining what remedy will accomplish the most fair and just result between the petitioner, the respondent, and the public. The standard for review of this element is easy to state but difficult to define in abstract terms. It is simply the standard of "abuse of discretion." In theory, the appellate court does not think the

problem through *de novo* and impose its decision
as if no decision had been previously made by the
trial court. It will instead evaluate the decision
of the trial court to see if it falls so far from the
mark of accomplishing maximum fairness and
justice between the three interests as to amount
to an *abuse of discretion.*

In King v. Saddleback Junior College District,
425 F.2d 426 (9th Cir. 1970), for example, a student petitioned the court to enjoin the college
from enforcing its dress code by refusing him
registration because of the length of his hair.
The district court granted a preliminary injunction. On appeal, the circuit court addressed itself
to "the narrow question of whether or not the
grant of the order is an abuse of discretion."
The court weighed the interests of the parties as
disclosed by the record:—the minimal inconvenience to the petitioner in having to comb his hair
above his eyebrows or wear a headband to meet
the dress code; the interest of the college in
managing its own internal affairs; and the lack
of impact on the public—and decided that the district court's decision had been so out of keeping
with a result that would be fair and just to the
relative interests of the parties that it was in fact
an abuse of discretion.   The order granting the
preliminary injunction was reversed.

C. APPEAL OF INTERLOCUTORY INJUNCTIONS

The standards for reviewing the findings of fact, rulings of law, and discretionary elements of interlocutory injunctions are the same as those discussed above for reviewing any other form of injunction. There are, however, certain rules that apply peculiarly to the review of interlocutory injunctions.

1. AUTOMATIC STAY AND WRIT OF SUPERSEDEAS

The effect of a *mandatory* interlocutory injunction—that is, one that alters the status quo (as defined in Chapter V above)—is automatically stayed as soon as an appeal is taken. A *prohibitory* interlocutory injunction—that is, one that preserves or restores the status quo—on the other hand, remains in full effect during the pendency of an appeal.

To reverse this automatic effect (i. e., to stay a prohibitory injunction or to continue a mandatory injunction), it is necessary to take the affirmative step of petitioning the appellate court. In order to stay a prohibitory injunction, the respondent would, in most jurisdictions, apply to the appellate court for a *writ of supersedeas*. He is usually required to file a supersedeas bond to indemnify the petitioner against harm caused by the stay.

To override the automatic stay of a mandatory injunction on appeal, the petitioner would ask the appellate court, in effect, to issue it's own mandatory injunction along the same lines.

The elements of an appellate court's decision to issue a mandatory interlocutory injunction or a writ of supersedeas are practically identical to those that enter into a decision by the trial court to grant or withhold an interlocutory injunction. One difference might be that an appellate court would generally accept findings of fact made by the trial court on the strength of oral testimony as a basis for its decision.

2. MOOTNESS

While the granting or denial of an interlocutory injunction is usually held to be appealable because of the finality of its practical effects on the interests of the petitioner and respondent, this appealability can be affected by the doctrine of mootness. Since, almost by definition, interlocutory injunctions arise in rapidly changing situations, it is often possible for the circumstances between the petitioner and respondent to shift abruptly prior to appeal, so that an injunction previously issued or denied would lose all relevance to the situation, and the issue on appeal would become moot. For example, in Dakota Coal Co. v. Fraser, 267 F. 130 (8th Cir. 1920), state authorities seized control of coal mines in North Dakota to prevent strikes that were threatening to have a serious effect on the public welfare. The mine owners sought a preliminary injunction against the seizure, which was denied. The mine owners appealed the denial, and during the pendency of the appeal, the state authorities withdrew from the mines after reaching an agreement with the owners. There seemed to be no threat of return by the state authorities. The Appellate Court, therefore, dismissed the appeal on the ground that the issue was moot and that the court would have no power to issue a pure statement of law that would have no direct effect on any controversy between the parties.

There is, however, one *caveat* to this rule. The respondent will not be allowed to use the doctrine of mootness to deprive the court of the power to grant relief by deliberately taking precipitous action to accomplish the irreparable injury that the petitioner seeks to prevent before the Appellate Court has a chance to rule. For example, in Ives v. Edison, 124 Mich. 402, 83 N.W. 120 (1900), the petitioner owned an easement in a stairway on the property of the respondent's lessor. The respondent sought permission to remove it and replace it with a different type of stairway in a different location. The petitioner refused permission; and on the respondent's threat to proceed anyway, the petitioner filed a bill for an injunction. The trial court denied the injunction, and the petitioner appealed. While the appeal was pending, the respondent tore down the old stairway and built a new one. The Appellate Court refused to allow the respondent to deliberately deprive it of power because of mootness as long as there was some possible relief that it could afford the petitioner. The court, therefore, entered a mandatory interlocutory injunction, ordering the respondent to rebuild the original stairway.

CHAPTER IX

EPILOGUE

A. SUMMARY

Of all of the legal systems devised for the dual purpose of accomplishing justice and fairness between litigants, and at the same time promoting the kind of respect for the court system that induces private citizens to entrust the outcome of their disputes to it, it is perhaps fair to say that none is more capable of achieving these goals than the system of equity. It has steered a careful course between the two major obstacles that have hobbled other systems of law. On the one hand, it has remained free of the kind of rigid, unyielding rules that have characterized the legal system in its attempt to conform all controversies before it to a one-dimensional standard of relief. The flexibility of the equity system was, in fact, born of the frustration of litigants who found that the legal system in all of its rigidity had nothing to offer them in aid of their specific problems. Through its years of development, equity developed rules and principles that would allow for growth and imagination in solving conflicts in unforeseen areas. This ability to grow and expand in unanticipated directions has made the equity system invaluable in keeping remedies abreast of newly recognized interests, particularly in such fields as civil rights, rights of privacy, and regulation of business activities.

On the other hand, flexibility can be overdone to the point of arbitrariness and unpredictability. The equity system carefully avoided this pitfall by developing rules and principles sufficiently tight to check a judge's discretion within reasonable bounds and to give form and stability to the system. Yet this was accomplished while the system remained pliable enough to allow a judge to mold the remedy to fit the problem, rather than force the problem to fit the confines of a remedy. The equity system is one of the very few ever to strike this delicate balance successfully. In short, the *system* is a marvel of craftsmanship and evolution.

But *systems* do not decide cases or issue orders. Between the system and the result lies the human factor, the judge, who makes the system succeed or miscarry. The system can only place the right tools in the hands of the judge, and from that point on, the result depends on the quality of the man. No system on earth places such demands on the wisdom, imagination, and conscience of a judge. Under a judge equal to the task, rights that might otherwise never be more than concepts *can* be translated into practical, visible results by means of a wisely tailored order to a respondent to act or refrain from acting. On the other hand, the system places undeniable power in the hands of the judge, and that implies the possibility of *misuse*, as well as *use*. The possible sources of misuse are almost innumerable—the favoring of special interests such as occurred in cases of "midnight injunctions" in the labor field; failure to apply all of the concern, knowledge, or imagination demanded by the case; or even the simple lack of the mental or moral qualifications for the demanding position of judge.

The system itself may not be quite perfect. Like any system that has evolved historically, it clings too tightly to the past in certain areas (such as the remnants of pre-occupation with property interests); but relatively few current miscarriages of justice can be attributed to defects in the system. The vast majority originate in human shortcomings. As the number of areas increases in which the only feasible solution to problems lies in injunctive remedies—such as pollution, discrimination, and unlawful business practices—the need for judicial quality increases concomitantly. Perhaps one answer can be found in increased specialization among judges at the action level of dispensing equitable relief. While this might seem to be an extravagant luxury at a time when a major problem in most busy jurisdictions is lack of an adequate number of judges, the proposal is worthy of serious consideration in view of the special demands placed on a judge sitting in equity and the critical nature of the judge's contribution to the functioning of this important system. The measure of success of this perfectly adequate system in defusing a number of serious points of increasing friction and tension in society will be directly proportional to the quality of performance of equity judges, and any step that will have an important effect on the upgrading of that performance should weigh heavily against the cost.

*

INDEX

ABSTENTION
See also Equity Jurisdiction
Constitutional rights, 120
Discretion, 118 f.
Federal courts, 119 f.
Political question, 121 ff.

ABUSE OF COURT PROCESS
Civil litigation, 52 f.
Criminal prosecution, 49 ff.
Multiple suits, 54 f.
Unfair advantage, 54

AD REM
See Parties

ADEQUATE REMEDY
See also Irreparable Injury
Abuse of court process, 49 ff.
Administrative procedures, 37
Civil litigation, 52 f.
Confidential relations, 42 f.
Criminal conduct, 60 f.
Criminal prosecution, 49 f.
Damages immeasurable, 43 f.
Dangerous remedy, 48 f.
History, 34 ff.
Insolvency of respondent, 46 f.
Intangible rights, 43 f.
Interlocutory injunctions, 157
Land interests, 39 f.

APPEAL—Continued

ARTISTIC PERFORMANCE
See Unenforceable Decree

BALANCING THE EQUITIES

BOND

BUILDING AND REPAIR
See Unenforceable Decree

[*255*]

498-2851